Gardens and Cultural Change: A Pan-American Perspective

Gardens and Cultural Change: A Pan-American Perspective

Gardens and Cultural Change: A Pan-American Perspective

Gardens and Cultural Change: A Pan-American Perspective

D1312186

Dumbarton Oaks Colloquium in Garden History

Held at Dumbarton Oaks, October 24–26, 2003

Gardens and Cultural Change: A Pan-American Perspective

edited by Michel Conan and Jeffrey Quilter

Dumbarton Oaks Research Library and Collection
Washington, D.C.
Distributed by Harvard University Press, 2007

Published by Dumbarton Oaks Research Library and Collection and
Spacemaker Press. Distributed by Harvard University Press, 2007

Library of Congress Cataloging-in-Publication Data

Gardens and cultural change : a Pan-American perspective / edited by Michel
Conan and Jeffrey Quilter.
      p. cm.
  "A colloquium held at Dumbarton Oaks, October 24-26, 2003"--T.p. verso.
  ISBN 978-0-88402-330-2
  1. Gardens--Symbolic aspects--America--Congresses. I. Conan, Michel,
1939- II. Quilter, Jeffrey, 1949- III. Dumbarton Oaks.
  SB470.7.G37 2007
  712.097--dc22
                                    2007038456

Printed in China

Contents

Introduction: *Gardens and the Construction of Cultures in the Americas*　　　3
Michel Conan and Jeffrey Quilter

The Chinampas of the Valley of Mexico　　　9
Saúl Alcántara Onofre

Gardens in the African Diaspora: Forging a Creole Identity in the Caribbean and the U.S.　　　29
Catherine Benoît

An Ideological-Aesthetic Approach to Buenos Aires Public Parks and Plazas　　　47
Sonia Berjman

Parks and Democracy in a Growing City: Palermo, Buenos Aires　　　65
Daniel Schavelzon

The Small Parks in New York City and the Civilizing Process of Immigrants at the Turn of the Twentieth Century　　　87
Rachel Iannacone

Contributors　　　105

Index　　　111

*Gardens and Cultural
Change: A Pan-American
Perspective*

*Gardens and Cultural
Change: A Pan-American
Perspective*

*Gardens and Cultural
Change: A Pan-American
Perspective*

*Gardens and Cultural
Change: A Pan-American
Perspective*

Gardens and the Construction of Culture in the Americas

Michel Conan and Jeffrey Quilter

Why do Western commentators find it so difficult to acknowledge the symbolic value of space? Why do they fail to observe how gardens sometimes allow their makers and their users to engage creatively with the symbolic value of garden spaces in their efforts to dwell poetically in the world? There are several reasons for this situation. Contemporary Western culture is deeply penetrated by the geometric understanding of the world that is part of the creative thinking of the industrial world. And, in turn, technical thinking has pervaded the bureaucratic practices of public management allowing in particular the manipulation of people that is part of modern states' ideologies. According to these views space is a deep seated abstraction shared by all human minds, an innate geometry that enables us to engage with the world. It is a pre-condition of our relationship to the world, and as such it lies beyond any intellectual control, beyond any critical inquiry into the transformation of symbolic qualities of space. And yet, despite this supposed neutrality of space, historical studies constantly demonstrate that space is at the heart of political struggles. It is striking to see, in Saúl Alcántara's chapter for instance, how quickly the Spanish invaders understood that the ability of the Aztec gardeners to move their floating gardens, the *chinampas*, across the lake of Tezcoco gave them an undue liberty to escape tax, and imposed the plantation of trees that rooted their gardens to the bottom of the lake.

Moreover, garden studies take their origins in art and architectural history. There are very good reasons for that, and much research on gardens remains to be done in these disciplines. They focus on gardens made with great art for some kind of public display. These gardens are studied and conserved, whenever possible, as objects, in a continuous struggle to prevent the life of nature and the erosion of rainwater, wind and animal life from destroying the appearance of immobility granted to them by historic representations. The quest for the retrieval of a past moment in the history of a celebrated place seems to discourage attention for the changing role of gardens in society, and for their role in cultural change itself. Yet, many of these gardens have been witness, and agents in great cultural changes, and sometimes heavily transformed as a consequence of the dynamics they supported. Moreover, gardens may exist and play an important role in cultural change without any relationship to the artworld, while others may claim to be artwork and contribute as well to other aspects of social life, to its economy, ethics, or politics. In fact gardens are places that seem to be open to indefinite cultural re-interpretation. But, at the same time, it is a common observation that we always have a sense of permanence when visiting a garden. Fresh flowers, old trees, rocks and statues all seem ageless. The continuity of natural and vegetable life may hide the discontinuities of social or cultural functions of a particular garden space. So, we should expect broader attention for the cultural and economic uses of gardens to reveal some aspects of gardens that remain unseen when art history is the main focus of inquiry. It may even reveal aspects of historic gardens of great interest for art history which have escaped attention. It might even eventually explain the odd course of garden art history when compared to the history of other arts, and the historical debates about the place of garden art among the Fine Arts. It seemed clear in the nineteenth century that the arts could be divided into arts concerned with either time or space, and since gardens were considered an art of space, attention was devoted to their spatial design.

Turning attention to the American continent one is compelled to recognize the importance of the symbolic role of space for many ancient people engaged long before their encounter with Western cultures. It could take many different forms. Fernando Santos-Granero has told the story of a trip he took through the Andes with a mountain native. As they walked his guide pointed to features of the landscape explaining how they related to the mythical and historical past of his tribe and his family. This landscape located him within a long line of generations linking almost seamlessly mythical time and contemporary family events. He derived a sense of self from these spaces, and walking a foreigner through the landscape amounted to introducing him into his life. Pursuing his investigations Santos-Granero observed that "Southern Arawaks anchor their sense of place in mythical narrations that recount how the shapeless space of pre-social times was transformed into their present-day territories through the activities of traveling creator gods and goddesses."[1] Their lives are rooted in a sacred landscape that they keep alive through ritual practices, thus making the landscape and its history part of their self identity. It is striking that whenever they migrate they transfer the landscape of origin into the new territories through naming and relocation of traditional rituals. Fernando Santos-Granero underlines that "the appropriation of new territories always involved the creation and reproduction of emotional links between the people and the land; that is, the production of locality as a "structure of feeling."[2] In his studies of the foundation of new settlements by migrating Aztecs just before and after the conquest by the Spanish, Angel Julián García-Zambrano has shown how specific landforms where selected to choose the space of a new settlement in order to reproduce features of space in mythical narratives of human origin.[3] These accounts call our attention to the verticality of space highlighted by Gaston Bachelard.[4] This verticality results from the unity of physical and metaphysical features embodied in space that enables individuals to derive their identity from the permanence of spaces mirroring their place in a cosmology. It is clearly not the same in every society or even in every place, since the physical and metaphysical features of space can vary greatly for different cultures. Maria Elena Bernal-Garcia proposes that the same physical place could be conceived and used as a different space by Aztec people under normal life circumstances and when undergoing a shamanic experience. Then the north-south orientation of space and the flow of time would be reversed, allowing people engaged in a shamanic ritual to travel back in time to the northern countries of origin while walking southwards during a day.[5]

The cultural use of spaces which present such striking symbolic properties allowed construction of landscapes on a grand scale linking cities and sacred mountains, and different cities to one another. The significance of these man-made landscapes is not yet understood even though they are well documented by archaeologists. It raises questions about the existence of gardens and their potential significance in these different cultural contexts. We know that there were ceremonial gardens in several ancient cities of the Inca and the Aztec empires, and that there were thousands of floating gardens on the lake of

Tezcoco, and yet we know very little about them, their uses, their significance for the lives of the gardeners and the communities where they were located. We would like to know whether they were part of the construction of collective identities, of the reproduction and transformation of the cultures of migrating people, and whether they contributed not only a meaningful grounding of self but also "structures of feeling" enabling people to share in some emotional dimensions of life.

When we engaged in this project we hoped that many Andean anthropologists and archaeologists would respond to these questions and contribute to a renewal of garden studies in South America. It did not happen, but we were fortunate to receive studies of garden developments in Mexico and Argentina as well as in the Caribbean and the United States that demonstrated the links between garden construction and cultural changes. Moreover, historical documents enable scholars to retrace the political circumstances of garden creation and the transformation of their uses and significances, thus giving modern historians the potential to see how gardens could be sources of resistance to domination as well as civilizing instruments in the hands of powerful institutions. Thus gardens appear as culturally defined spaces where some social changes are produced and contested.

Gardens appear as places where a population can establish the material and symbolic support for its continuous and stable existence. This is clearly evidenced by the examples given by Saúl Alcántara Onofre and Catherine Benoît about two completely different populations of gardeners: the *chinamperos* of Aztec origins around the remainders of the lake of Tezcoco, and the descendants of slave families in the Caribbean island of Guadeloupe. Their approaches are quite different. Saúl Alcántara Onofre is mostly concerned, in "The *Chinampas* of the Valley of Mexico," with documenting the practices of garden cultivation and their resilience to large changes in the urban environment of Mexico that threatens their existence. Catherine Benoît attempts to discover in "Gardens in the African Diaspora: Forging a Creole Identity in the Caribbean and the U.S." the role of garden development in the construction of a "Creole" identity. She suggests that slaves and their descendants created garden space in an effort to survive terrible conditions of oppression. This resulted in a development of their own culture and a sense of cultural identity rooted in specific garden practices. She proposes further that the transmission and the reinterpretation of these garden practices along the lines of generation is part of the process of construction of modern "Creole" identities in the context of a racially and politically divided society. She proposes that ritual garden practices inscribe the lives of individual members of the family in the lineage of their ancestors and contribute to their spiritual welfare and their bodily health. There are two themes that can be recognized in these two contrasting approaches. First, both insist on the importance of a deep and well documented understanding of the material construction of garden spaces, of gardening and garden practices, and of the garden roles in family economy. Second, they both show that traditional garden cultures are subjected at present to re-interpretations and transformation by the conjunction of the tourist industry and of the changing economic and social conditions of the gardeners themselves. They diverge in their interpretation of garden conservation: Alcántara calls for a heritage protection by the state, while Benoît exposes the fallacies of the reinterpretation of vernacular gardens as botanical conservatories that French state policy of heritage conservation encourage.

This divergence of interpretation calls for more research on the role of the state and of its ideologies in the management of gardens for public use. Two Argentinian authors, Sonia Berjman and Daniel Schavelzon engage in a dialogue on this question by examining, from different points of view, the history of public gardens in Buenos Aires. Their debate is interesting because it proceeds from similar approaches but differs in the interpretation of the cultural context. Sonia Berjman proposes a long history of the development of public spaces and gardens by European colonizers in "An Ideological-Aesthetic Approach to Buenos Aires Public Parks and Plazas," stressing the egalitarian principles and practices they introduced into city life. She stresses a consensual view of Buenos Aires society. She shows how it supported the introduction in Buenos Aires of Western models in a permanent quest for modernity (looking to Spain in the eighteenth century, to France at the turn of the nineteenth century and to the United States at the end of the twentieth). She carefully documents the choice of models to be imported, of designers made responsible for new projects and the results of their action. Thus public spaces seem to be simply a mirror of changes taking place elsewhere, either in other Western countries or within local government and popular tastes and fashions. Daniel Schavelzon takes a closer look in "Parks and Democracy in a Growing City: Palermo, Buenos Aires," concentrating his attention on the history of a single park. He shows how a newly elected city governor, Juan Manuel de Rosas (1793-1877), created a new kind of public park around his residence, breaking away from any existing design tradition, in order to promote a new form of social life in the city. He further explains how his demise led to the destruction and reconstruction of this park by his successor, Domingo F. Sarmiento (1811-1888). His analysis prolongs the discussion of design issues by Berjman. However, it also provides the reader with an understanding of some social issues that the two governors faced. His study of spatial changes, and the resistance and controversies they triggered illustrate both the ideological content of the projects, and the symbolic value vested to public space by different social groups. His perspective acknowledges the dynamics of social and cultural differences within the city of Buenos Aires, and attempts to reveal how public space embodied ideological commitments that divided the local population.

This perspective is shared by Rachel Iannaconne's presentation of "The Small Parks in New York City and the Civilizing Process of Immigrants at the Turn of the Twentieth Century." Like Schavelzon's study of Palermo park, it builds upon a detailed study of a two-pronged design process, each combining in a different way social and aesthetic concerns of the municipal government. She not only acknowledges the cultural, social and economic differences that separate the immigrants from the mainstream population in New York City at the beginning of the twentieth century, but she also highlights the internal division between rulers and professionals inside the local government. They all share a view of public park space as an instrument for civilizing immigrant populations in the hands of local government. They disagree, however, on the civilizing features of landscape architecture. Iannaconne presents the contending theories of the agency of park space among city professionals. More interestingly, she also analyzes the conflict between reformers and the contending theories of spatial agency. Far from considering garden space as a neutral ground, some of these reformers defended its role in the formation of the personality: "The ownership of an individual plot and confining that owner's care to that one plot, in short time develops selfishness in the children. This is overcome by requiring from each and all a general care of this whole garden, such as paths, decorative flower beds and grass, so uniting individual ownership with a responsibility for the appearance of the whole, making a foundation for good citizenship." (Parks Department 1910, 51) Needless to say such theories are unwarranted, and they only mirror a disciplinary project entertained by some social reformers. However, the history of the demise of landscape architecture for small public parks in New York City demonstrates the importance of theories of space and of its symbolic power to influence the attitudes and behaviors of citizens entertained by municipal reformers. It is a great pity that we do not know more about the actual reception of these parks by all their users.

As a whole this book highlights new issues that demand more research, and it also demonstrates that from Argentina to the United States some scholars are coming to terms with the same questions and asking similar questions about gardens. It becomes clear as we proceed that an understanding of the dynamic significance of garden spaces demands both a study of the production and the reception processes. It also deeply suggests that the relationships between the two processes are mediated by complex political processes to which professional ideals and debates only contribute indirectly. This is to say that an understanding of changes in garden design demands going much beyond a study of design ideas themselves. Schavelzon's and Iannaconne's analyses suggest that attention should also be paid to conflicting attitudes towards park space in a city, and that design ideas should be placed within the context of studies of political action in the city.

These perspectives, however broad they may seem, might lead us to forget that they only concern a limited aspect of the questions that we raised at the beginning of this introduction. They tend to cast in a new form the questions raised by the history of garden and park design, as if space were a homogeneous matter, like air or water, which is identical for all humans whatever their culture or their mode of engagement with nature. Much research is necessary at present to empirically investigate this question. It seems from the presentations by Alcántara Onofre and Benoît that scholarly studies of gardening practices and of the role of gardens in the life cycle of people still steeped in some non-Western cultural tradition could offer a refreshing source of discussion for all garden studies. We hope that American scholars will find in these pages inspirations and questions that will encourage them to contribute to such a renewal of the domain of garden studies.

Notes

[1] Personal communication by Fernando Santos-Granero from the Smithsonian Institution on "Arawakan Sacred Landscapes: Emplaced Myths, Place Rituals and the Production of Locality in Western Amazonia" at Dumbarton Oaks, May 10, 2002.

[2] Personal communication at Dumbarton Oaks, May 2002.

[3] Angel Julían García-Zambrano, "Ancestral Rituals of Landscape Exploration and Appropriation Amongst Indigenous Communities in Early Colonial Mexico," in Michel Conan, ed, *Sacred Gardens and Landscapes: Ritual and Agency*, Dumbarton Oaks Colloquium Series in the History of Landscape Architecture (XXVI). Washington D.C.: Dumbarton Oaks, 2007.

[4] In Gaston Bachelard's writings verticality is a recurrent theme, with which he engaged in some of his deepest reflections on the poetics of dwelling space in the first chapter of his *Poetics of Space*, entitled "The house from cellar to garret." This book constitutes a phenomenological study of imagination, which he conceived as a "concrete metaphysics" deeper than the metaphysics studied by philosophers such as Heidegger to whom he alludes. Bachelard proposes that, beyond all practical activities, dwelling in a house is an imaginary response to the function of construction: "The dreamer constructs and reconstructs the upper stories and the attic until they are well constructed. And, as I said before, when we dream of the heights we are in the rational zone of intellectualized projects. But for the cellar, the impassioned inhabitant digs and re-digs, making its very depth active. The fact is not enough, the dream is at work. When it comes to excavated ground, dreams have no limit" (Bachelard 1994, 18).

Bachelard, however, did not restrict his study of verticality to the poetics of the house space. In another book devoted to the poetics of air he wrote: "Verticality is not an idle metaphor: it is an ordering principle, a law of mental activity, a scale along which degrees of a specific sensitivity can be experienced. As a whole the life of the soul, all the subtle inner emotions, all hopes, all fears, all the moral forces that concern the becoming of men have a vertical component, in the mathematical sense" (my translation of Bachelard 1996, 16).

Joanne H. Stroud notes in "The Future of Beauty: Gaston Bachelard as Guide,": "Bachelard wrote a separate (book) on the attraction of the flame of a candle. Here, his interest is specifically focused on the upward thrust of the flame that invites reverie in a vertical direction. Perceiving the connectedness of all things, of all creatures, is the action of an earthly, horizontal linkage. It is possible to participate in a vertical connection, either upward or lower, a connection which unites heaven and hell. The beauty of the universe can pull one in a horizontal awareness but more often into a verticalizing mode, leading to an invitation to transcendence." In: www.dallasinstitute.org/Programs/Previous/FALL00/talktext/jstroud.htm; May 08, 2007. Bachelard, Gaston. *The Poetics of Space*, translated from the French by Maria Jolas with a new foreword by John R. Stilgoe. Boston: Beacon Press, 1994. Bachelard, Gaston. *L'Air et les Songes*. Paris: Le livre de poche. Biblio-Essais, 1996.

[5] María Elena Bernal-García, "The Dance of Time, the Procession of Space in Mexico-Tenochtitlan's Desert Garden," in Michel Conan, ed, *Sacred Gardens and Landscapes: Ritual and Agency*, Dumbarton Oaks Colloquium Series in the History of Landscape Architecture (XXVI). Washington D.C.: Dumbarton Oaks, 2007.

Gardens and Cultural Change: A Pan-American Perspective

Gardens and Cultural Change: A Pan-American Perspective

Gardens and Cultural Change: A Pan-American Perspective

Gardens and Cultural Change: A Pan-American Perspective

The Chinampas of the Valley of Mexico

Saúl Alcántara Onofre

Chinampa: The Gardens in the Water Landscape

The term *chinampa* derives from the *Náhuatl "chinamitl,"* which means reed boundary or hedge, or a fence with sticks or intertwined reeds; the Spaniards called them *camellones* or *sementeras*. In general they were of large proportions, so that the owner could build his dwelling in the central and most solid area. The pristine meaning of *chinampan* ("in the fence or fenced land")

probably refers to the sticks placed around a floating piece the land built as a raft, focused on the production of the *almácigos,* little germination compartments that functioned like a greenhouse in order to generate different sorts of harvests, such as vegetables and flowers. A basic characteristic of the *chinampa* cultivation system is that canals located between the artificial islets not only serve as circulation passages but also for the provision of water. This arrangement results in an extraordinarily fertile and highly productive agricultural pattern.

Chinampas were cultivated—and still are—in some areas of the existing lakes of the Valley of Mexico. Planting is done in special earth beds, called by the Spaniards *almácigos,* which permit a maximum use of available space, where the seeds germinate and the plants start

Fig. 1. Xochimilco aerial photo, 2004, courtesy of Armando Alonso Navarrete from Programa Universitario de Estudios Metropolitanos, Universidad Autónoma Metropolitana, Xochimilco.

to grow rapidly. A *chinampa* is rarely laid to rest (Fig. 1).

The use of aquatic vegetation as fertilizers, or other organic fertilizers, make possible an intense production year after year, given a favorable climate and a constant humidity of the soil through continuous irrigation. Shelter against the elements such as winds, frost, overexposure to sunlight were taken into consideration by building a roof made of *petate* (palm matting) or hay on the top the *almácigos* area, providing individual care to each plant.

That great productivity of the *chinampas* was complemented by easy transportation of grown products by water along main canals; probably the most important was the famous Canal de la Viga, which connected lakes Xochimilco, Grand Tenochtitlan and Texcoco. That water route provided a direct access for these products to the center of Mexico City (Fig. 2).

Fig. 2. Holiday on La Viga, Waite photo, 1905, Archivo General de la Nación, México.
Fig. 3. Flowers stroll Canal de la Viga, Waite photo, ca 1905, Archivo General de la Nación, México.

Chronicles of Spanish conquistadors mention hundreds of canoes or *piraguas* loaded with maize, beans, calabash, chia, vegetables and flowers produced in the *chinampas* of Xochimilco arriving daily to the Aztec marketplace. Four hundred years later, *chinampas* still provide part of the vegetables and flowers that Mexico City consumes. In recent years, areas of *chinampa* production have been alarmingly reduced (Fig. 3).

Since the sixteenth century, diminished *chinampa* production was associated originally with the conquistadors' policy to dry up the lakes for two reasons: firstly, to protect their palaces, monasteries or convents; secondly, their greed to obtain more building territory for different purposes. Nowadays, this diminishing is related to the gigantic spread of the city that has invaded agricultural areas in Xochimilco and Chalco. Furthermore, the water springs that used to feed lakes have been redirected for use of the inhabitants of the region, leaving the *chinampas* above ground and dry. Another issue we have to consider is the attraction of cultivators to find more stable jobs in the city. Consequently, a good number of productive *chinampas* have been abandoned, forming a sadly desolate landscape. The growth of the city has created new non–agricultural jobs in urban services and industry, which have been occupied principally by inhabitants of the rural areas (Fig. 4).

In consequence, certain actions are required for the conservation and rehabilitation of sites where *chinampa* cultivation practices still take place. Planned protective management of the 11,138 hectares of surviving *chinampas* (of which 390 are public property) might well include: raised water levels, water decontamination, land regulation ownership, recovery of the ancient cultivation systems, and safeguarding the historic and artistic heritage they represent. This collection of streets, houses, churches, plazas and parks represent approximately two hundred blocks of urban area.

This urban area, Xochimilco, the main *chinampa* town in the Valley was declared a World Heritage Site in 1985 by the United Nations Educational, Scientific and Cultural Organization (UNESCO) . Unfortunately, only twenty percent of this declared land still produces. Due to this concern, it is important to include Xochimilco in the World Heritage At-Risk List (Fig. 5).

Historical Survey: Tenochtitlan, A City in the Lake

If we take a look at history, the Aztecs or Mexicans were the last of a long list of migrant groups who settled in the Valley of Mexico, during the twelfth and thirteenth centuries, leaving Tenochtitlan last of all the prehispanic cities that existed in the Valley. Before the foundation of the Aztec City, the Aztecs lived two years in Iztacalco, before passing to a small island, where they found a *"nopal cardón Opuntia streptacantha* upon a stone, and on top an eagle" (Clavijero 1853, II, 60). The Mexicans named the city Tenochtitlan or Mexico (*Tenochtitlan* means "place where there is a *nopal* on the top of a stone"), and started to build the sanctuary of Huitzilopochtli or Mexitli, their guardian deity.

Fig. 4. Water fountains near Xochimilco, Waite photo, 1905, Archivo General de la Nación, México.
Fig. 5. Currently chinampa' area 2005, courtesy of Armando Alonso Navarrete from Programa Universitario de Estudios Metropolitanos, Universidad Autónoma Metropolitana, Xochimilco.

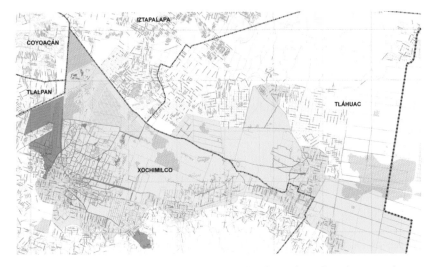

The ancient city of Tenochtitlan, established by the Aztecs on a small island in the middle of the lake area of the Valley of Mexico, according to tradition in 1325 under their first king, Tenoch, offered excellent means of defense and food supply, thanks among other things to the existence of the *chinampa* system, which overcomes the inconveniences of a swampy terrain always threatened by potential flooding.

The first major problem the ancient Mexicans had to cope with was a severe shortage of land to build their houses; the island was too small for the population. Several chroniclers agree that they built stockade areas where the lake floor was lowest and produced embankments with rubble and water vegetation, which little by little permitted them to link their island with other neighboring islets, and gradually expand their habitable space (Fig. 6).

Fig. 6 Xochimilco, high way, trajineras and chianampas, anonymous photo, ca 1907, Archivo General de la Nación, México.
Fig. 7 Xochimilco the Venice of Mexico, Waite photo, 1905, Archivo General de la Nación, México.

Tenochtitlan: The Landscape During the Conquest

In 1520 Hernán Cortez entered the city via the causeway of Iztapalapa, which led directly to the Aztec metropolis from the southeast. To put it in terms of a conqueror, what surprised the Spaniards most about Temistitlan, and about other towns around the lake, was its placement as well as the surrounding mountain landscape and the vast flat areas occupied by the two main lakes of Texcoco and Xochimilco. (Cortez, in his *Cartas de Relación,* constantly makes reference to the city as *Temistitlan,* which must surely be a paleographic mistake, as he most probably wrote *Tenustitlan.*). One of these lakes is fresh water, and the other which is greater, is salt water.

As Cortez himself narrates:

They are divided by a small cuadrillera (o. Sp. for cordillera) with very steep hills and these lakes come together in a strait in the

*plain, which forms between these hills and the high sierras, this City has
many plazas, where there is a continuous market and
business of buying and selling.*

*It has another plaza as large as two times the City of Salamanca, all
enclosed by portals, where every day there are above seventy thousand souls
buying and selling. There is an alley of herbalists, where there are all the
medicinal roots and herbs that can be found in the land… and the honey
of plants that in the other islands are called maguey, which is much better
than syrup, and from these plants they make sugar and wine, which they
sell as well. They sell much maize in grain and bread, which much excels,
in the island as on the main land* (1960, 78), (Fig. 7).

Montezuma's kingdom produced great buildings, both within and
outside the City, surrounded them with gardens and forest, some of them
survived many years after the conquest. Today the sacred groves of
Chapultepec subsist, as do a few other landscape vestiges of that period.

Fig. 8. The willow trees Salix bonplandiana symbolize the god Tezcatlipoca, smoking mirror, 2006, (photo: author).

Hernán Cortez, Bernal Díaz del Castillo and the Anonymous
Conqueror mention that the majesty of Moctezuma was reflected also in the
greatness and splendor of his palaces, his houses of leisure, and his parks and
gardens. The palace where he usually resided was a vast building made in masonry, with twenty doors that led to the town square and
the surrounding street (this property was located in the Zócalo where the Palacio Nacional is located). It boasted three patios, with a
great fountain in one, and more than a hundred rooms. Cortez confessed that nothing similar existed in Spain.

The historian Clavijero writes that of all the above mentioned palaces and gardens little survives apart from a few groves in
today's Chapultepec park… that have been conserved by the viceroys for their pleasure […] the Spaniards, after the conquest ceased
caring for the royal gardens, laid waste the forests and reduced the land to such a state, that at this day the magnificence of that king
could not be believed were it not for the testimony of those that annihilated [his regime]" (1853: III, 100).

The new city was laid down following a regular grid plan. In the new streets, some of the original canals were kept
while others were filled in with the debris of the vanquished city. Where the canals were kept the streets were called "water
streets." On the outskirts, beyond the limits of the Spanish-renaissance city, however, nearly all streets developed irregular happy-
go-lucky patterns, in such a way the Mexicans were forced to adapt in strange ways to be able to subsist. A proffered alternative
was a *chinampa*. As Lake Texcoco was saline, the soil used in the *chinampas* was useless for cultivation; nonetheless, with constant
washing with water from the lake itself, these salts were partly shed away, permitting cultivation at reasonably productive levels.
The historian Humboldt (1966, 39) mentions that some of these artificial islands in Lake Chalco were towed with ropes or
maneuvered with long poles, in a sort of punting technique, from one place to another with great ease, as one would move a
canoe. But when the first land registry was made by the Spaniards, it became necessary and mandatory to declare for the register
only the *chinampas* fixed with *Ahuejotes* trees *Salix bonplandiana,* as it would have been impossible to plot and establish the legal
limits of the moving allotments (Fig. 8).

limits of the moving allotments (Fig. 8).

Father Diego Durán states that with the election of the first Mexican king, Acamapichtli, king Tezozomoctli of Azcapotzalco, master of the island where the tribe settled, elevated the tribute levels the Aztecs had paid until that time, demanding, among other things, that…"they should deliver grown sabinos Taxodium mucronatum and willows Salix bonplandiana for planting in his town, and that they should build a floating raft (chinampa), and they should plant on it all the vegetables of the land, maize, chile, beans, squash, chards, etc." (1984: II, 57-58).

Ococaltzin by advice of their god Huitzilopochtli, told the Mexicans to obey…. "and they took the raft floating on the water, all planted with corn already with ears, end chile, and tomatoes, and chards, beans, squash and roses; after seeing it, not without great admiration, Tezozomoc said to his people: this seems to me, brothers, something more than human, because when I ordered it, I had it almost for an impossible thing" (Durán 1984, II, 58). An identical version appears in the codex Ramirez, which derives from the same source as above, makes reference to "a plantation on the surface of the lake, which moved as a raft" (Leicht, 376). In Tezozomocs' Chronicle the following tribute is described:

> with dawn of another day, Teomama had everything laid in order as he had it placed on the camellón [floating orchard or flower bed], they loaded corn, whole green corn, seasoned, and chile, tomatoes, squash, beans, and also a live snake and a royal duck lying over her eggs, and the Mexicans towed it, as everything was a lake with water, up to the limits of Azcapotzalco….and the third time….they were told….for the third they should bring a camellón or chinampa covered with rushes, and in it bring a heron lying with her eggs; and in the camellón should come a royal duck with her eggs….and so the Mexicans took the camellón with the heron, the royal duck and the coiled snake (1943: 232).

The Jesuit José Acosta made good use of these same sources, and reproduced them in his *Historia Natural y moral de las Indias,* which was published in 1590. It refers to the floating beds in the same manner:

> …a cultivated plot that is built in the water and drawn along in the water, and adds: those who have not seen the plots that are made in the lake of Mexico, right in the water, will have this as a hoax, or at most will believe that it was an enchantment of the devil that these people worshipped. But in reality of truth it is a very practicable thing, and one that has been done many times, to make a cultivated plot that moves in the water, because earth is laid on sedge and rushes, and on top of it plants are sown cultivated, and they grow and mature, and it is taken from one place to another (1962, 167-68).

Somewhat later the Dominican father, Fray Hernando de Ojeda, influenced by Acosta but without making reference of the legend of *Acamapichtli*, wrote in 1608:

> ….in this lake the indians use some very noteworthy things that are moveable orchards about twenty and thirty feet in length and of whatever width they want, set in the water upon turf, rushes and reeds, on which they plant

places; and in this manner they take them held with ropes from one place to another in the lake (Ojeda quoted by Armillas, 1983: 163).

The Franciscan Fray Alonso Ponce, who traveled throughout New Spain between 1585 and 1587, mentions the same practice. After discussing fixed (static) *chinampas* at length, he adds that "the indigenous people also put maize almácigos on these chinampas [static] and from there they transpose them [to other plantations], which is something very particular of that land." (Ponce quoted by West y Armillas, 1983: 100). Very different from these floating *chinampas* mentioned by other authors that transported *almácigos* are the "true" *chinampas* according to Father Ponce:

Fig. 9. Great canal on Ciénega Grande, 2006 (photo: author).

Of these acequias (irrigation ditches) there is an infinite number in Xuchimilco, where there are also many houses enclosed by water, and to reach them and to go to the milpas (cultivation fields) that they have inside the lake, they use canoes. These milpas grow corn, chile and chia Genus salvia […] . these milpas are called chinampas, and they build them in the water, joining and heaping turf and loam from the same lake, and making very narrow strips, as they do in Spain when they distribute council lands, leaving an acequia between strip and strip or between chinampa and chinampa, while these rise above the water around a vara (0.838 meters) or less, and carry a powerful maize because with the dampness of the lake it grows and sustains itself, even if water does not fall from the sky (Ponce quoted by West and Armillas, 1983: 100) (Fig. 9).

Torquemada doesn't report specific information about the mobility of the *chinampas,* but he mentions the preoccupation of the peasants of this New Spain for aquatic issues regarding augmentation or diminishing of water levels in the lake:

It is said of those that live in the fresh water lake that surrounds this City of Mexico, that without great effort they plant and harvest their maize and their cabbages, because everything is on camellones, which they call chinampas, which are strips built on the water and enclosed by ditches, so that they do not need to be watered, and the less the waters from the sky, the greater will their breads be; because too much water drowns and sickens them (Torquemada quoted by Sanders, 1983: 162).

Fig. 10. Flowers, trajinera and Chano's chinampa, 2006 (photo: author).

According to Franciscan Father Vetancurt such gardens (mobiles or static) could be also found along the streets of ancient Mexico City: "other (streets), all of them waterways, which corresponded to the rear sides of the houses, with camellones, on which they plant, called chinampas…." (Vetancurt quoted by Leicht, 1937: 378). On the other hand, Fray Toribio de Benavente (Motolinía) mentions "small infill orchards with acequias, as they had them in times of their heathenism, in different quarters of the City" (2001: 229).

Torquemada is not the first to translate the word *chinampa* for *camellón*. Father Durán earlier wrote of a spy, hiding in a mass of reeds, who suddenly…came "out to some camellones, dry land in the vicinity of Culhuacan." Further on he mentions that in the mythical Aztlan the forefathers of the Mexicans "used to make camellones on which they planted maize, chile, etc." (Durán, 1967: 92).

Even today the camellones are made in the same way, and Rafael García Granados writes that "….the indian owners of the chinampas (presently veritable islands) day by day make them grow at the expense of the canals by forming new stockades around them, and filling in the gaps with earth they extract from the bottom" (1934, 338).

Stakes were used not only for building *chinampas* but also for building the causeways that connected the city with firm land. For example, father Duran mentions relating to the causeway that led to Xochimilco, which the method of building it was to set stones and earth drawn from the bottom of the lake, as well as turf, on top of a great amount of stakes. In the gardens of the Iztapalapa there was a great pond, and bordering it there was an ample footpath, and according to Cortez, "towards the wall of the garden, everything is fashioned with reeds and horizontal yards" (Cortez, 74) (Fig. 10).

The first to identify cultivated rafts with *chinampas* was the Jesuit Priest Francisco Javier Clavijero in his *Historia Antigua de México,* 1780, (1853, 395) having mentioned the subject two times: firstly, paraphrasing Acosta's passage he refers to the legend of Acamapichtli, calling the raft "a great floating orchard," and underlining, as Gemelli Careri also did, that he personally saw "the very beautiful gardens that until then have been cultivated on the water" (Clavijero, 1853: 167). The second passage reads as follows:

the Mexicans, throughout the long pilgrimage they undertook, starting from their native land of Aztlan up to the place where they founded Mejico, always tilled the earth in all the places where they stopped, and they lived from their harvests when oppressed by the Colhuas and the Tepanecas, and when the Mexicans were reduced to inhabit the miserable lagoon island, they ceased for a few years to cultivate the land, because they had none, until trained by necessity and by industry, they formed movable fields and orchards, floating on the waters of the lagoon. The manner in which they built them then, and which is still observed today, is very simple. They make a wattle with reeds and root from certain lake plants to build a support for the earth for the garden. On this foundation they lay light sods of the types that swim in the lagoon and over everything the slime they retrieve from the bottom of it. Their regular figure is that of a quadrangle; length and width vary, but

Fig. 11. *Chinampa* with xacalli or house, like in ancient times, 2006 (photo: author).

commonly have, I believe, around eight toesas (a toesa is an old Italian unit of measure, equivalent to 1.946 meters) in length, no more than three in width and less than one foot in elevation above the surface of the water. These were the first fields that the Mexicans had available after the foundation of Mexico, on which they cultivated maize, chile and other plants necessary for their sustenance. Later on, having multiplied it self in excess flourished, due to the hard work of that people, gardens with flowers and odorous herbs appeared, which were employed in the cult of the gods and for the delight of the rulers. Presently flowers are cultivated, and all sorts of vegetables; every day of the year, with the break of dawn, one can see innumerable canoes moving along the canal to the great square of that capital city, laden with many sorts of flowers and aromatic herbs that were cultivated in those orchards. They grow admirably there, because the mud from the lagoon is very fertile, and does not require water from the sky. In the larger fields one usually finds a shrub, and also a hut where the cultivator can take refuge and defend himself from the rain and the sun. When the master of an orchard, or as it is more vulgarly known, a chinampa, wishes to move to another place, or move away from a pernicious neighbor, or come nearer to his family, he can get into his canoe, and by himself, if the field is small, or with the help of others if it is large, takes it on tow to wherever he pleases, together with the hut and the shrubs. The part of the lagoon where these orchards and gardens are to be found is a most delightful place of enjoyment, in which the senses receive the sweetest pleasure of the world (Clavijero, 1853: 167), (Fig. 11).

On the other hand, Clavijero mentions that the beautiful city of Xochimilco—the largest, among the courts, of all those in the Mexican Valley—was founded on the shores of lake Chalco, a little more than twelve miles from the capital. Its population is very numerous, its temples many, its buildings magnificent, and particularly its beautiful floating gardens, from which it took the name of Xochimilco, (Clavijero, 1853: 10, 281) which means the "place of gardens and flower fields."

Contemporary *Chinampas* Situation

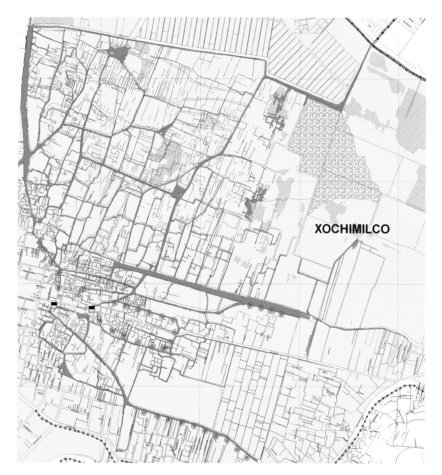

Fig. 12. Hydrographic Situation of Xochimilco, 2005, courtesy of Armando Alonso Navarrete from Programa Universitario de Estudios Metropolitanos, Universidad Autónoma Metropolitana, Xochimilco.

In spite of everything, the *chinampas* constitute one of the main sources for the cultivation of vegetables and flowers in Mexico City, especially during spring and winter. Yet, the number of active *chinampas* has been notably reduced. A great part of the old lakebed still conserves farming water landscape of the fixed *chinampas*, especially in San Gregorio Atlapulco and San Luis, but many canals are dry, and the fertile vegetable compost layers are scarce, so that the fundamental traits of the *chinampa* cultivation system based on continuous planting and irrigation are no longer possible.

This unfortunate circumstance is a consequence of the accelerated growth of the Mexico City Conurbation Area, which today contains more than twenty three million inhabitants; with the growth of the city, the Valley has increasingly dried up. The largest part of water that came from the volcanoes and fed lakes such as Chalco, Xochimilco and Texcoco, has been channeled directly to the city, leaving the *chinampas* with few possibilities for survival.

Of the great *chinampa* areas of Iztacalco, Santa Anita, Iztapalapa, Mexicalcingo and Culhuacán nothing is left, everything is totally covered by urban construction. The *chinampas* of Tláhuac and the Mixquic survived until recently, and Xochimilco, the queen of the *chinampa* communities, is now almost completely dry; the Xico – Chalco, the chinampa zone no longer exists, (Fig. 12).

A *Chinampa* Construction Process

It is important to explain that ancient Mexican farmers showed great creativity using the resources at hand in order to build the *chinampas*. The sweet-water lakes Xochimilco and Chalco were partially covered by a thin layer of floating vegetation, both dead and alive, composed mainly of varieties of *tule Thypha sp.*, water tall grass, and water lilies *Nimphaca sp.* These plants were used as construction materials to form a sort of floating cushion of varying thickness (from twenty centimeters to one meter), capable of holding the weight of a person. This thick layer is known locally by the names of "lawn", "strip" or *atlapalácatl* (knitted layer of water tall grass and water lilies).

Chinampas are usually built on swampy sites or permanently flooded areas. In order to form a *chinampa,* a foundation is established, that is, the bottom is punted with a pole until a shallow point is found to establish the foundation of a fixed *chinampa*; the next step consists of establishing the limits of the new *chinampa* with long reeds or shafts (Fig. 13).

Dimensions vary from three or five meters wide by sixty to ninety meters long, and sometimes more; these last ones are not frequent, but could be found in Iztapalapa in the sixteenth and seventeenth century. A medium area needed to build a *chinampa* is in the range of ninety square meters. The size is in direct proportion to the foundations and the width is always small, with the object of permitting an easy watering of the center of the *chinampa* by casting the water from the canal, and of securing constant humidity through filtration.

Once the foundation is established subsequent layers of "lawn" and black earth are spread, until the island is formed. The "lawn" can be separated from its natural position by cutting with shovels or *coa* (wooden knife), until portions are liberated and set afloat. Sometimes the earth for the new *chinampa* is taken from older ones, which have grown too high for appropriate irrigation and cultivation, due to a constant addition of subsequent layers. The original soil is extracted from the bottom of the canals, between *chinampas*. It is usually unproductive if it is covered by water, or has an unusually large content of it, but will quickly upgrade as it dries and mixes with other materials (Fig. 14).

This cultivation system can be

Fig. 13. Recovering with poles the limits of the *chinampa*, 2006 (photo: author).
Fig. 14. Looking for mud in the bottom of the main canal, 2006 (photo: author).

considered as the most productive compared to those traditionally practiced in the country. The cultivation area is small in relation to the amounts of labor and capital employed in its exploitation. The soil is not allowed to rest one single month in a year; as soon as a plant is harvested another one is planted or transplanted, in such a way that when one part of the *chinampa* is being planted or transplanted, the other is being harvested. One astonishing aspect of this cultivation system is that the entire

Fig. 15. Willow trees, flowers on the restored *chinampa*, 2006 (photo: author).
Fig 16. Mr. Chano's *chinampa*, 2006 (photo: author).

surface of the *chinampas* is cultivated, not only the surface but also the four sides (in the case of a mobile *chinampa*). In this case the sides were cultivated with roundhead cabbage.

The mud that is extracted from the canal and laid on the *chinampa* is usually mixed with water lentils, called *chichicastle,* hacked water lilies *Iris spuria* and other aquatic vegetation, and left to rot. This mixture is known as *mojada* (or washing), and will take seeds that do not need *almácigo* preparation, such as radishes *Raphanus sativus L*, onions *Allium cepa L.,* carrots *Daucos carota,* lettuce *Lactuca sativa L.,* cabbage *Brassica oleracea var. botrytis L.,* etc.

When a *chinampa* in process of formation has reached a height of twenty or twenty five centimeters over the water level, the edges are planted with willows *Salix bonplandiana,* in Mexico commonly called *ahuejotes* or *huejotes.* The stakes in form of threes are planted at a distance of four to five meters, and on sprouting generate a very beautiful landscape, where one can appreciate a lush cultivated area set among a series of very slender trees, in a single, unique composition. The Mexican willow happens to be thinner than others. Therefore, the shading could be controlled (Fig. 15).

Lessening of *Chinampa* Areas in Mexico City

Apparently the oldest *chinampa* area is to be found in the lakes Chalco and Xochimilco, to the south of the valley. When the Mexican immigrants built the *chinampas* for the first time in the places allotted by Tezozomoc, they only copied a technique already in ancient use in the valley. Several viceroyal documents indicated that *chinampas* existed near Azcapotzalco and Popotla, in the northwest section of the actual Mexico City, but now only a few vestiges remain. Likewise they existed in the area between the Tlacopan causeway and the southeast side of Chapultepec hill. Since viceroyal times and up to the early beginnings of the twentieth century, a line of *chinampas* extended from the southeast quarter of San Pablo, in Mexico City, towards the south along the Canal de la Viga, passing by Santa Anita, Iztacalco and Mexicalcingo, up to the town Culhuacán, towards the east. During the government of Porfirio Díaz in 1910 the Canal de la Viga was already abandoned and partially closed, leaving the surrounding areas without water. Nonetheless around Iztacalco the *chinampas* still kept their original form up to a few years ago and were cultivated by using water pumped from the subsoil. By the middle of the twentieth century *chinampas* still existed in nine towns: Xochimilco, Nativitas, Acalpixca, Atlapulco, Tlaxialtemalco, Tulyehualco, Tláhuac, Tetelco, Tezompa and Mixquic, all on lake Xochimilco – Chalco (Fig. 16).

Thanks to numerous mountain springs on the eastern and southern borders of the valley, pouring into lakes Chalco and Xochimilco, abundant water was always at hand for the *chinampas*. Because of this, they survived for a time, when artificial draining of the lakes began around the beginning of the last century. But since 1948, the smaller canals of Tláhuac and Mixquic have dried up.

Chinampa Cultivation Techniques

Disposition of the almácigos

To form the *almácigos* or nursery plantation (in *Náhuatl* known as *tlachtli,* or a layer of mud), lake

Fig. 17. Finishing the seed bed or *almácigo*, 2006 (photo: author).
Fig. 18. Seed beds (*almácigos*) on the Chano's *chinampa*, 2006 (photo: author).

muddies are mixed with aquatic plants, the results trod on until as a fine mass it can be rendered flat and smooth with a shovel or even with a mason's trowel. The thickness should be either five or ten centimeters, so that one can cut the mud cake into cubes of five by five or ten by ten centimeters, according to the type of sprout one intends to plant, and in the center a hole is made with a dibble, in which the seed is inserted; this dibble, generally made of a corn cob is driven to a depth of half a thumb. After the seeds have been laid, a fine layer of black earth or a compost of pulverized cow dung is spread, to cover the whole

Fig. 19. Chapines (plant cubes) product of the seed bed, 2006 (photo: author).
Fig. 20. Chapines (plant cubes) dislocate, 2006 (photo: author).

aquatic plants, the results trod on until as a fine mass it can be rendered flat and smooth with a shovel or even with a mason's trowel. The thickness should be either five or ten centimeters, so that one can cut the mud cake into cubes of five by five or ten by ten centimeters, according to the type of sprout one intends to plant, and in the center a hole is made with a dibble, in which the seed is inserted; this dibble, generally made of a corn cob is driven to a depth of half a thumb. After the seeds have been laid, a fine layer of black earth or a compost of pulverized cow dung is spread, to cover the whole plantation. This serves a double purpose: it covers the seeds and, entering the slits made by the previous cutting process, keeps the cubes intact, so that when the transplant period arrives, the cubes can be separated one by one without hurting the roots of the neighboring shoots (Fig. 17 and 18).

Transplanting the almácigos

When the time comes for transporting the *almácigos* from one *chinampa* to another place, the cubes (called *chapines*) are separated to facilitate the removal, a knife or a small wooden shovel is used to separate them without cutting the roots at the shoots. Then each plant is sent to its proper destination, either for human consumption if a vegetable or to sell as a product in the case of flowers or ornamental plants (Fig. 19 and 20).

Precautions against bad weather conditions

Fig. 21. Protecting the seed bed with straw and reed (photo: author).
Fig. 22. Transport of mud by piragua canoe, 2006 (photo: author).

the *almácigo* is small. When the *almácigo* is larger, *petates* are also used (Fig. 21).

Soil recycling

Soil recycling is recommended, due to the presence of salts in the earth coming from the waters along the canals and its subsequent alkalinization. These factors combined with the drying action of the sunlight have regrettable effect on the soil, which is little by little rendered unproductive and must be periodically removed. To do so, the farmer will first check the condition of the soil in the *chinampa*, and replace it, if possible, with new earth or mud.

With a hoe the earth is broken up and thrown back into the canal and new earth is brought from other areas in the vicinity, usually extracted from neighboring canals; if this is not possible, the same earth is again taken out of the canals, and it is left to rest for a while to eliminate excessive salts. The best time to fertilize the earth is during the soil recycling process by adding extra layers of aquatic vegetable material (Fig. 22).

Irrigation systems

It is not necessary to water the *almácigos* in the chinampas because the base and the roof perform an extra function as greenhouses. In the case of the roof, the water vapor formed from the original dampness of the earth condenses and precipitates again, thus maintaining the constant humid environment proper for the first stages of the young plants' development. The irrigation is complemented by the absorption of the humidity provided from the canals to the *chinampa*.

Fig. 23. Seed beds, canal and willow trees, 2006 (photo: author).
Fig. 24. Lettuce seed bed, 2006 (photo: author).

When the *chapines* (germination cubes) are transplanted from the *almácigos* to the field, irrigation will be required. This is done with an instrument made with a long pole, on the end of which a wooden hoop is attached from which dangles a rawhide skin to form a sort of large spoon, called a *cuero* or "leather." This scoops water on the planted areas. This method is also used for the extraction of mud from the bottom of the canals, when needed. The transplanted *chapines* are irrigated every three or four days, according to weather conditions. This operation has two advantages: firstly, it procures water for the plants, and secondly, it also allows constant fertilization of the earth by extracting the water with sediments. In Xochimilco watering is done, at present, with manual sprinklers. In certain cases, as with parsley, *romeritos*, thyme and some flowers, small ditches are made square to the line of the canal, ending in a circular hole for depositing water. In this way water can be distributed to any point on the *chinampa*. Sometimes, instead of plain water, liquid mud or suck is deposited, which has the advantage of retaining humidity for a longer time (Fig. 23).

Production of the *Chinampas*

The *almácigo* cubes for green chile *Capsicum annum* or small peppers are usually two fingers in size, and the seeds are planted by the end of September; the cubes for tomatoes *Phisalia* are two and a half fingers in size and are planted in October. The squares for *jitomate Lycopersicum esculentum* are three fingers wide and are planted in October. The pumpkin seed *Cucurbita mixta* requires squares three fingers wide; they are planted in the first days of February, covered not with fine earth, but only with dry *zacate* (high grass). The *zempoalxóchitl Tagetes* is planted in squares four and half fingers wide, during April to celebrate the day of Saint Mark. In past times poppy flowers *Papaver rhoas* were planted, and two harvests were obtained in a year. Planting is done on the day of Saint Augustine, to be able to cut during lent. The flowers were between three and ten centimeters in diameter and often had two sets of petals; the *almácigo* squares for poppies were two fingers wide.

An interesting aspect of the cultivation of these flowers is that they require their protection roofs facing west. The following flowers were also cultivated: carnation *Dianthus sinensis,* daisies *Callistephus chinensis L., pensamientos Viola tricolor L. var. hortensis,* chrysanthemum *Crisantemunn indicum,* and dahlias *Dahlia variabilis.* The vegetables least resistant to frost—chile *Capsicum annum L.,* peas *Lathyrus adoratus L.,* tomatoes *Lycorpersicon esculentum Mill*—require protective roofs in all cases. The parsley seeds *Petroselinum sativum* are planted in August. Two varieties of cabbages *Brassica oleracea,* are planted in the *chinampas,* one of which is called *verdulera* or vegetable vendor, which is planted on the day of Saint John and harvested in December; the other, *repollo Roundhead cabbage,* is not planted with seeds but rather transported in shoots rising on the root that remains after the grown cabbage head is cut. Plants of lesser importance are: radishes *Raphanus sativus L.,* beans *Phaseoulus vulgaris L.,* cucumbers *Cucumis sativus L.,* pumpkin *Cucurbita mixta pang,* carrot *Daucus carota,* and different herbs.

The maize *Zea maize* is usually planted in this manner: the *almácigos* are laid out as already mentioned and the shoots should be protected by roofs, as this plant is not very resistant to frost. In time the *chapines* with small plants are transported to furrows on the *chinampa,* so that a small harvest can be obtained. These plantings are very successful on the *chinampas,* so harvests are taken long before they are in normal fields (Fig. 24).

The Cultural Landscape in Xochimilco

The origins of the Xochimilco landscape can be set long before the arrival of the Spaniards. The combination of inventiveness and capacity of the Xochimilcas, who were able to redeem artificially formed land from the lake to create a very peculiar form of agriculture, must be considered one of the pillars in the development of the Aztec and other neighboring cultures in the Valley of Mexico.

Xochimilco constitutes a region which in the twentieth century still followed the simple traditional methods that could be found in places as far away as fifteenth-century Central America. Thanks to its benign climatic conditions, intensive cultivation does not affect the quality of the soil, nor diminish its nutrients. Year after year production of vegetables and flowers is abundant.

The huts of the mainland were formerly made of *adobe* and covered with thatch. In the canal district, they were usually made with reed walls and reed or thatched roofs, and are known as *jacales,* a word deriving from the Aztec *xacallis,* which means straw hut. The floor areas were between four and twenty square meters.

Traditionally, the Indian shows little interest in concentrating parcels; on the other hand, if one *chinampa* is as fertile as another, there could be the possibility of interchanging or merging both. A piece of land that a person has cultivated and that has been owned by his father and grandfather, will not be sold or changed needlessly for another that has no meaning for him. The result of this attitude has been the conservation of the indigenous distribution of parcels in their original form.

The great antiquity of the *chinampa* system is clearly demonstrated by their representation on maps dating from the time of the conquest. In these maps the lakes are shown partially covered by *chinampas,* and later maps show them covered almost completely. In present days the number of *chinampas* has diminished dramatically with the disappearance of the lakes. Thanks to the *chinampa* system the cultural landscape of Xochimilco is unique, and holds a very special place in relation with other horticultural systems developed in different regions of our planet. In earlier times lakes Xochimilco and Chalco were one considerably larger water body, but were separated by a dike that also served as a causeway (used by Hernán Cortés in his first

Fig. 25. Different seed beds almácigos in a chinampa cultivation system, 2006 (photo: author)
Fig. 26. Transport of dahlias by piragua or canoe, 2006 (photo: author).

Intensive cultivation in the artificial gardens was originally based on a strict division of labor within the extended family. Since the introduction of cattle and the plow represented no advantage for agriculture in Xochimilco, in this region the great *Hacienda* or ranch systems did not prosper. Only a few small farms with limited numbers of cattle, together with dry-land agricultural produce, were able to survive as long as the original indigenous population and their unique agricultural methods were the main factors shaping the landscape.

Yet, because of the great beauty of its landscape, *Xochimilco* is still one of the favorite recreation areas for the inhabitants of the big city. One can still find small flatboats painted with screaming colors and covered with garlands made with fresh flowers for hire for excursions along the existing canals. On Sundays and holidays, such as the March festivities in which "the most beautiful flower of the community" is elected, the canals are seen filled with boats loaded with visitors and musicians.

The urban layout of Xochimilco changed little during the centuries of Spanish domination. In the center lies the ancient renaissance church, commanding the main square of the town, with its great trees and green areas; on the sides of the square one finds government buildings, a covered market and a few other lesser constructions. Around this central nucleus the city spreads uniformly, forming a grid pattern which earlier included only a few blocks, but now has grown to absorb the surrounding communities, each with its own traditions and its own local church.

A few viceroyal houses still survive. Some have a second floor, but most have only a ground floor surrounding a central patio, which gives access to all rooms. As the visitor walks away from the center of the town and goes into the indigenous quarters, a street gets narrower and finally ends up a path among the dwellings, passes over a few bridges, and ends suddenly at the edge of a canal.

It can be said that after the conquest, there were no more drastic external changes in the landscape, apart from the slow fall of the water level of the lakes; in those times Xochimilco presented a very characteristic agricultural landscape, which owed its appearance almost exclusively to the hand of man. The lakes of Xochimilco and Chalco were nourished by a great number of water springs from the southeast portion of the valley; nevertheless, there were three unfortunate decisions that definitely changed the water landscape during the presidential period of Porfirio Díaz. First, the drainage works for the Valley of Mexico finished in 1900. Second, the decision to dry up the remaining lakes. Third, the fact to tube the water from the springs of *Cerro de la Estrella* for human use in Mexico City, in 1903.

All the facts mentioned above provoked the slow but generalized fall in surface and aquifer water levels in the Valley as a whole. The result of the new drainage and tubing the water was evident, the total elimination of water traffic on the Canal de la Viga, and the main causeway for the movement of the *chinampa* products to the city.

According to Elizabeth Schilling (1983, 71), in spite of the existence of "Regulation for the Conservation and Keeping of Lake Xochimilco" (before 1938), the water levels of the canal have kept falling and the artificial islet has increasingly emerged from the water. With such low water levels, the fertilization and watering practices using the traditional methods are gradually being abandoned (Fig. 25).

In this way, one can observe the slow extinction of the last of the five lakes of the Valley, and by extension its canals. If something is not done soon to check this sad situation, the *chinampas* will in little time be dry and the soil will be ready to be used in other urban activities instead of agriculture activities, and the dead canals will signify the end of an era of the Aztec cultivation system. New land use forms will be introduced, and these ancient indigenous landscapes will disappear, to be replaced by a grim parody of a monstrous incontrollable sprawl of the Mexico City urban region (Fig. 26).

Bibliography

Alvarado Tezozomoc, Hernando. *Crónica Mexicana*. México: Editorial imprenta Universitaria, 1943.

Armillas, Pedro. *Jardines en los pantanos* in *Agricultura chinampera*. México: Editorial Universidad Autónoma de Chapingo, 1983.

Careri, Gemelli. *Viaje a la Nueva España*. México: Universidad Nacional Autónoma de México, 1976.

Clavijero, Francisco Javier. *Historia Antigua de México*. México: Navarro Editor, libros del I al X, 1853.

Cortés, Hernán. *Cartas de Relación*. México: Editorial Porrúa, 2002.

De Acosta, José. *Historia Natural y Moral de las Indias* México: Fondo de Cultura Económica, 1962.

De Benavente, Toribio. *Historia de los Indios de la Nueva España*. España: Editorial Dastin, S. L., 2001.

De Sahagún, Bernardino. *Historia General de las cosas de la Nueva España*. México: Editorial Porrúa, 1981.

Díaz del Castillo, Bernal. *Historia verdadera de la conquista de la Nueva España*. México: Editorial Porrúa, 2002.

Durán, Diego. *Historia de las Indias de Nueva España e Islas de la Tierra Firme* México: Editorial Porrúa, Tomo I, II: 1984.

García, Granados, Rafael. *Xochimilco*. México: Monografías Mexicanas de Arte, Vol. 5, Talleres gráficos de la Nación, 1934.

Humboldt, Alejandro de. *Ensayo político sobre el reino de nueva España* México: Sepan Cuentos, 1966.

Leicht, Hugo. *Chinampas y Almácigos Flotantes* México: Anales del Instituto de Biología, editorial: UNAM, 1937.

Ponce, Alonso. *Colección de Documentos Inéditos para la Historia de España*, España: Tomos I y II Imprenta de la viuda de Calero, 1873.

Sanders William T. *El lago y el volcán: la Chinampa* in *Agricultura chinampera*. México: Editorial Universidad Autónoma de Chapingo, 1983.

Schilling, Elisabeth. *Los "jardines flotantes" de Xochimilco* in *Agricultura chinampera*. México: Editorial Universidad Autónoma de Chapingo, 1983.

Wets, Robert and Armillas, Pedro. *Poesia de los "Jardines Flotantes"* in *Agricultura chinampera*. México: Editorial Universidad Autónoma de Chapingo, 1983.

Gardens and Cultural Change: A Pan-American Perspective

Gardens and Cultural Change: A Pan-American Perspective

Gardens and Cultural Change: A Pan-American Perspective

Gardens and Cultural Change: A Pan-American Perspective

Gardens in the African Diaspora: Forging a Creole Identity in the Caribbean and the U.S.

Catherine Benoît[1]

In the travel accounts of his postal mission to the West Indies in the 1860s, Anthony Trollope expressed surprise at discovering that the Jamaican landscape was only partly composed of sugarcane fields. Visiting there a little more than twenty years after the abolition of slavery in the British West Indies, he noted further that the larger part was made up of forests and provision grounds:

> It is of course known that the sugar-cane is the chief production of Jamaica; but one may travel for days in the island and only see a cane piece here and there. By far the greater portion of the island is covered with wild wood and jungle — what is there called bush. Through this, on an occasional favorable spot, and very frequently on the roadsides, one sees the gardens or provision-grounds of the negroes. These are spots of land cultivated by them, for which they either pay rent, or on which, as is quite as common, they have squatted without payment of any rent. These provision-grounds are very picturesque. They are not filled, as a peasant's garden in England or in Ireland is filled, with potatoes and cabbages, or other vegetables similarly uninteresting in their growth; but contain cacao-trees, breadfruit-trees, oranges, mangoes, limes, plantations, jack fruit, sour-sop, avocado pears, and a score of others, all of which are luxuriant trees, some of considerable size, and all of them of great beauty. The breadfruit-trees and the mango are especially lovely, and I know nothing prettier than a grove of oranges in Jamaica. In addition to this, they always have the yam, which is with the negro somewhat as the potato is with the Irishman; only that the Irishman has nothing else, whereas the negro generally has either fish or meat, and has also a score of other fruits besides the yam. The yam, too, is picturesque in its growth. As with the potato, the root alone is eaten, but the upper part is fostered and cared for as a creeper, so that the ground may be unencumbered by its thick tendrils. Support is provided for it as for grapes or peas. Then one sees also in these provision-grounds patches of sugar-cane.[2]

Fig. 1. "View in Old North Sound. Antigua," Engraving by Reeve after drawing by J. Johnson from N°1 of a Series of View in the West Indies, 1827. Yale Center for British Art, Paul Mellon Collection.

Eighteenth and nineteenth-century travel accounts, essays and poetry are crammed with descriptions expounding on the picturesque quality of Caribbean landscapes and slave gardens. Recently literary critics have shown how the aestheticization of labor in the descriptions of the eitghteenth and nineteenth centuries British West Indian and Saint-Domingue plantation landscape through the use of the pastoral and georgic tropes of arcadia, eden, bounty and paradise conceal the work and the labor force that produce the landscape.[3] Figure 1 entitled "View in Old North Sound. Antigua" drawn by J. Johnson in the beginning of the nineteenth century, is a representation of an Antiguan estate that aims to provide plantation life with a sense of serenity, order, and abundance.[4] By depicting luxuriant gardens while an old African man rests under the shade of a tree and younger ones work peacefully, this type of representation credits an understanding of plantation life as serene and peaceful. The view shows the estate of Captain Freeman in the division of Old North Sound.

Despite the rhetoric of most descriptions one finds sparse but original details that convey a sense of the gardens' role for the plantation economics and for the enslaved Africans' relation to the environment. Mention of garden locations, time allocated to their cultivation, lists of plants, different names of plants (European, Creole names or the ones given by the enslaved), and descriptions of garden rituals inform us not only about European perceptions of these tropical environments, but also about specific social and cultural practices that produced these landscapes.

In this chapter I will rely on literary and archeological evidence to argue that gardens have been privileged places for the development of personal and collective identities in the African diaspora since the beginning of the European colonization of the Americas. Enslaved Africans developed an original relationship to their natural and social environments through the development of their own horticulture in dooryard gardens and provision grounds. The gardens of all enslaved and free people of African descent introduced horticultural innovations contesting cultural, economic and political power relations at the heart of the plantation system. They were part of, if not conditions for, the construction of Creole cultures.

Origins and Development of the Gardens

The diversity of gardens and fields in the American plantations

The landscape of the plantation often pictured in texts is comprised of fields of sugarcane and in some cases of the Great House garden and its allees. The reality was far more diverse, however, and the hierarchy of relationships on a plantation was reflected in its landscape.

A plantation comprised three types of fields. First, there were the fields dedicated to the staple that generated the wealth for the plantation, such as sugarcane, cotton, coffee or rice. Second, there were the fields that provided crops for feeding both the free and enslaved populations living on the plantation, such as yam grounds[5] or manioc fields in mid-eighteenth century St. Croix,[6] and more rarely corn and bean fields. Additionally, on some plantations slaves were able to cultivate patches dedicated to one crop such as watermelon or potato in Piedmont, Virginia.[7] It seems that even in this case the fields were tilled by the slaves under the direction and supervision of the plantation's owner.

Besides the Great House gardens, two other types of gardens existed: the dooryard gardens usually referred to as yards, house plots, or kitchen gardens;[8] and the provision ground, referred to as mountain grounds, mountain lands,[9] negro grounds, or palinkas.[10] They were places where, unlike the fields, enslaved Africans' activities did not take place under the control of the planter or overseer.

In the slave quarters, the dooryard gardens that surrounded the slave cabins were private places where neither the owner of the plantation nor the overseer dared to come except perhaps in times of reorganization of slave quarters or when they were improving social control through the implementation of hygienic regulations. For analytical purposes I define the dooryard gardens as a set of relationships engendering different types of practices, either horticultural, social, or religious and not as the mere objectified physical space of the Cartesian tradition.[11] The dooryard garden is a place constituted by a set of relationships between the inhabitants, visitors, and the spirits of the dead, as well as plants and animals, and this may have been the case since the beginning of slavery. The dooryard gardens became places where slaves managed to develop a culture of their own: it is in the slave quarters and more specifically in these yards that such activities took place as cooking, worshipping one's gods and ancestors, meeting with neighbors, creating families, dancing and singing at night, and burying one's dead. The dooryard gardens were also places of cultivation, to supplement the produce of the provision grounds.[12] More rarely the gardens could be located in front of the slave quarters and they contained not only fruits and vegetables, but also flowers;[13] some plots of land could have been allocated at a certain distance from the slave cabin, but within the limits of the slave quarters.[14] In the islands of Barbados and Antigua where there was no room for provision grounds, dooryard gardens were more intensively used.[15]

The provision grounds, in which enslaved Africans managed to work on their free time, were generally located at the periphery of the estate in places unfit for fields, on the steep slopes of ravines,[16] or farther off in the mountains.[17] They provided crops that were part of or entirely constituted the slaves' diet. Eventually the products of these gardens were sold to other slaves, freed people and the planters, sourcing the development of markets in the Caribbean. These markets were usually held on Sundays. In the Caribbean, trade relations took place between islands: slaves living in St. John sold yams, tannier, or beans to slaves in St. Thomas;[18] the Cuban maroon communities traded with local haciendas but also with Jamaican and Dominican markets.[19] Attempts to forbid these markets led to upheavals.[20] Gardens and markets became part of what came to be called the "peasant breach," the "proto-peasantry,"[21] or the "slave economy,"[22] which enabled the development of the Caribbean peasantries after the abolition of slavery.

The Origin of the Gardens

Discussion of the origin of gardens in the Black diaspora of Brazil, the United States and the Caribbean has posited either an Amerindian or an African origin depending on the focus of the study: the technology required to exploit the gardens, the worldviews they refer to, and their economic role in the plantation system.

Botanists and agronomists studying gardens of the French Caribbean islands, either provision grounds or dooryard gardens, have emphasized the Native American techniques of gardening such as slash-and-burn agriculture, names of some plants, and some culinary techniques, to posit an Amerindian origin of the gardens.[23] The seventeenth-century missionaries' *Relations* (by the French missionaries Breton, Du Tertre, and Labat) in describing how Europeans and Africans in Martinique and Guadeloupe relied on the Amerindian knowledge of the environment, supplement this analysis. Yet neither botanists nor agronomists mention any African gardening techniques.

Art historians, anthropologists, archaeologists, and social scientists who have studied African-American yards in the Untied States and occasionally in the Caribbean, have defended an African origin of the garden layout, functions, uses, and meanings by isolating nineteenth and twentieth century cultural traits, by de-historicizing them and characterizing Africa as a timeless continent where all people share a unique way to relate to the environment.[24] The only theoretical model of transmission proposed is a set of ahistorical formal parallels and assumed meanings found on both sides of the Atlantic. Yet the descriptions proposed by these researchers for the slave quarters' yards in Virginia and the contemporary African-American and Caribbean gardens suggest the existence of a continuum of cultural forms within different regions of the Americas that demands further explanation.

Emergence of the Provision Grounds from the Atlantic Islands to the American Plantations

A more dynamic approach to the origin of the provision grounds is to look at them as part of the development of the plantation system in the Atlantic islands. Geographers and historians have looked at the spread of provision grounds from sugar plantations in the Atlantic islands to the Americas. The plantation system arose in the twelfth century in the Mediterranean Basin with the cultivation of sugarcane by a mix of free and enslaved labor forces. The production of sugar developed in Cyprus from the thirteenth century to the fifteenth century; then Sicily became the main sugar producer in the second part of the fifteenth century until the Italians finally introduced the production and commercialization of sugar in Portugal.[25] From there, the plantation system based on the work of enslaved labor for producing a specific crop (sugarcane, coffee or cotton) followed the expansion of the Portuguese colonial empire in Africa and in the Americas.

Although it is not possible to propose a history of the development of provision grounds in the Atlantic islands, John Thornton, in *Africa and Africans in the Making of the Atlantic World,* quotes two citations about the presence of provision grounds in São Tomé plantations as early as the 1520s.[26] That slaves had to produce their own food themselves seems to be characteristic of the plantation system. In some slave regions of Africa earlier in the sixteenth century, Thornton mentions how slaves had one day a week to toil for themselves.[27]

Provision Grounds in the American Plantations

Although the history of slave gardens still has to be undertaken, some historical steps are now established. When the Portuguese initiated a transatlantic slave trade in the 1530s with slave shipments direct from the Atlantic islands to the Caribbean and Brazil, the plantation system in both its economic and social dimensions was exported to the Americas. The first mention of provision grounds or dooryard gardens in Brazilian plantations, however, appears quite late in the sources. A description of Brazil under Dutch administration in 1647-1648 recorded that many plantation slaves had provision grounds on which they grew peas, beans, millets and maize when they got some rest after twelve hour work days.[28] The provision grounds existed in Brazil before this first mention in the 1640s. The practice of granting provision grounds to enslaved Africans is mentioned at the same time in Caribbean sources for Surinam, Barbados, Martinique and Guadeloupe and is attributed to the Dutch planters who left Brazil in the beginning of the seventeenth century for the Caribbean islands when the country was subdued again by Portugal.[29]

These gardens became part of the structural organization of labor in the plantations. Their development can be understood neither beyond the context of the planters' economy, nor outside the Atlantic world economies. It resulted from the master's exigencies, calculus and interests, and seems to have been based primarily on the broad market economics of sugar production. Planters' strategies for feeding the slave population were crucial to the development of these gardens. There were five ways to feed the population: 1) by importing food from the metropolis or the United States; 2) by having a non-slave population cultivating provision grounds outside the plantations; 3) by having common grounds cultivated by the enslaved; 4) by using a mix of imported and state-produced food, and; 5) by having the slaves produce for themselves. When sugar production was very profitable, planters preferred to have the enslaved population working in the fields, to feed them instead of giving them time to produce their own food. It seems that across the Caribbean, in the beginning of the plantation system, gardens were quite present; then at the height of staple production in the eighteenth century, some islands did not have these gardens and relied on imported food; when the decline in staple production began, gardens were cultivated again.[30] The situation was the opposite in Brazil where in times of high market prices the planters dedicated all their property to the cultivation of sugarcane and left the slaves responsible for their own food, cultivated on provision grounds at the periphery of the plantations.[31] Political events in the Atlantic world had a direct effect on the existence of provision grounds. During the American war of Independence 1775-1783, people were dying of hunger in the British West Indies islands which relied on food shipped from North America—food either grown on New England plantations or cod fished in the Atlantic. As a consequence, provision grounds had to be developed. After the end of the slave trade in 1808, planters could not afford to lose slaves to starvation, and encouraged the development of provision grounds.[32] Finally, in some islands, the existence of these grounds became dependent on metropolitan laws concerning food supplies for slaves: in the French colonies of Guadeloupe, Martinique and Saint-

Domingue, planters were required to import food from the metropolis. The number of laws passed that urged them to feed their slaves suggests, however, that they preferred to allocate plots of land to the slaves.[33] In the islands such as Barbados where the provision grounds were not so developed, enslaved Africans cultivated more intensively patches of land around their huts.[34]

The study of the origin of gardens calls for an integrated approach of technological exchanges, contacts, and borrowings between the different groups present in the context of the Atlantic economies. Several criteria should be distinguished in future research in order to understand the formation of the creole gardens: the emergence and the spread of the sugar plantation system from the Atlantic islands to the Americas, the work organization of the enslaved labor force, the organization of food production on the plantation, the origin of horticultural techniques, the origin of plants, and the worldviews of which they are part.

From Place to Space

In the *Practice of Everyday life,* Michel de Certeau has defined a space as the practice of a place, as the lived experience of a place.[35] Gardens as a place refers to the definition that we find in dictionaries: enclosures wherein vegetables, medicinal and ornamental plants are grown. But gardens are also spaces constituted by practices that define individual and collective identities. In the case of the Black diaspora, it is particularly relevant to look at practices in dooryard gardens. Many anthropologists have noticed how in the Caribbean or the Southern states of the United States, social life and family life take place more often in the yards than inside the walls of the house.[36] By looking at garden practices, we shall see how today, and arguably since the beginning of slavery, gardens gave birth to new ways of being in the world. Anthropology has considered the study of gardens as irrelevant for a long time, so there is a dearth of analyses to rely on for comparisons between different areas. From a historical perspective, the lack of documentation concerning labor organization for garden cultivation and social uses might explain why gardens have been so little studied; however, I agree with Tomich when he writes that "this lack of documentation is perhaps a mute testimony to the genuine autonomy that the slaves enjoyed in the conduct of these activities."[37]

Spatial Order and Social Control

In his archaeology of the organization and uses of space in Jamaica's Blue Mountains coffee plantations, James Delle has proposed a theoretical model to analyze the planters' control of enslaved Africans achieved through the organization of the plantation layout and use of space. Relying on the work of the geographer Edward Soja, Delle defines spatiality as the property of space to give rise to and result from social relationships. The spatialities of control are comprised of the spatialities of movement (they are the planters' attempts to control movement through space), and the spatialities of surveillance (they are the planters' attempts to control action through panoptic Benthamite surveillance).[38] In response to the spatialities of control, enslaved Africans developed spatialities of resistance. Delle proposes to consider the plantation hospital and the yaw house as such. There enslaved people could escape the plantation regime for a while. He also proposes that after Emancipation, land tenure—often of former provision grounds—offered a new form of spatiality of resistance. Land tenure marked the laborers' independence against the emerging industrialization of the agricultural economy.[39]

It is not so much the location of the slave quarters in relation to the Great House as the practices therein that define the spatialities of resistance. Numerous archaeological and historical studies have shown the diversity in plantation layout when considering the Great House location with respect to the work buildings and slave quarters. The slave quarters might either be hidden from the view of planters who preferred to look at their work houses or plantation landscape, or situated close enough to be in direct view from the Great House porch or back door. In Louisiana the difference reaches its acme in the examples of the Evergreen plantation—whose slave quarters are located far behind the Great House and are served by a large alley that a foreigner, as I was, could initially mistake for the plantation alley—and the Laura plantation, whose slave quarters are located only a few yards from the back porch and can be easily observed from the verandah.[40] Dooryard gardens and provision grounds were places that challenged the different spatialities of control. They were places where a Creole culture developed and is reaffirmed today. They were also spaces that developed in size and volume of activities in tandem with the development of creole culture.[41]

Through a meticulous study of one thousand Jamaican plantation maps available for the years 1750-1880, Barry Higman, who also excavated the Jamaican plantation of Montpelier, showed that the first criterion in laying out the Great House, the works, the fields, slave quarters and provision grounds, was not so much the spatialities of movement and surveillance as what he called "movement minimization" in the accomplishment of work tasks.[42] This became obvious by the beginning of the nineteenth century, for planters' writings even failed to mention the location of slave quarters. Higman interprets the planter's reduced concern with spatial control to be a consequence of the development of a Creole society in which enslaved Africans were perceived as less likely to want to escape the plantation. Higman also understands that environmental and topographical contexts have to be taken into account when studying the layout of the plantation in other islands. He noted than in Barbados, slave quarters in estates of smaller size seem to have remained integrated in the Great House-works complex.

For the most part, enslaved Africans were not allowed to choose the location of their quarters or influence the design of their cabins; they were, however, the builders and users of the housing facilities, which gave them some leeway to reinterpret and resist the architectural and spatial organization of the planters.[43] In a study of the Virginian planters' ideals in the design of nineteenth-century slave cabins and the uses of these dwellings, Larry McKee has convincingly argued that observations by some white observers that some cabins were "filthy" (containing the presence of refuse, weeds, and plants), which were confirmed by archaeological excavations, can be interpreted as slaves' resistance to planters' representations of cleanliness and order as a means of social control.[44] Archaeology has revealed the presence of root cellars in eighteenth century dooryard gardens of the U.S. Upper South. They were used for either storing food or concealing valuables. The ongoing conflicts between the planters and the people they enslaved translated into the constant struggle against the spatialities of control.[45]

The Gardens as Botanical Gardens
•Knowledge and Naming

Gardens were places where a Creole social life developed but also places where a Creole knowledge of plants of American, European, African, and Asian origin was constituted. Many of the plants that can be found in the Caribbean are of foreign origin and have been acclimated in the Americas following the European discovery of the continent.[46] Plants were transferred through a network of European botanical gardens and stations that were established in colonized territories and supervised by institutions that developed in the European metropolises. The transfer of plants from Europe to the Americas, and from the Americas to Africa and Europe through the role of institutions or well-known amateurs and explorers is well documented. The

Fig. 2. Luxuriance of a dooryard garden, Guadeloupe 1999. Photo by the author.
Fig. 3. Multi-storey cropping in a Guadeloupean garden, 2000. Photo by the author.

same is not true for the transfer of plants from Africa to the Americas. The botanical knowledge and agricultural and horticultural techniques brought by enslaved Africans to the Americas have just begun to be acknowledged.[47]

Since the beginning of slavery, dooryard gardens have been described as hodgepodges, "*salmigondis*" not only because their contribution to the landscape was judged picturesque, but also because they were considered a threat to the planters' conception of order and cleanliness. Contemporary writers, missionaries and writers insisted on the luxurious vegetation of these gardens, at least in humid climates, whose layouts were very different from the Great House gardens. These gardens were and are still places which have been considered as "botanical gardens of the dispossessed,"[48] and "miniature colonial botanical gardens"[49] (Fig. 2).

The knowledge that enslaved Africans had of the environment was acknowledged by many travelers and missionaries. "Natural histories" mention plants and trees by their European and Indian names, given by the enslaved, and the way different groups could use them for food or medicinal reasons. Enslaved Africans learned the uses of native plants through their contacts with Amerindians in situations where such contacts existed or by following the "functional substitution" principle from their former knowledge of African environments.[50] They experimented with plants that they discovered even before Europeans became interested in them, and planters discovered some African plants in the gardens of the people they enslaved.[51]

Plants from the gardens and forests were used for aesthetic, medicinal, and food purposes. A Creole medical practice anchored in precise representations of the body developed from this knowledge and experimentation of plants in the gardens. Archaeological excavations like Poplar Forest, VA have revealed the presence of plants that might have been used for medicinal purposes.[52] The knowledge of the medicinal uses of plants by healers of African descent provoked both admiration and fear in the planters who could themselves rely on this medicine.

Archaeological evidence has shown that cooking activities took place in the dooryard gardens and not inside the cabins. The analysis of vegetal and faunal evidence has shown the diversity of food resources that the enslaved had to rely on, such as gardening, hunting, foraging, and fishing, to compose meals that were rarely decent enough to sustain health. The same evidence has revealed which animal parts were consumed (usually the poorest ones), and how they were prepared (mainly in stews). This still characterizes main Creole dishes of the Caribbean in which, for example, pig feet or chicken necks are slowly cooked in a sauce that constitutes the basis of a meal. The same excavations have provided information about cooking utensils, revealing how food was prepared and eaten. All of this suggests the emergence of original cooking techniques, hence the development of a Creole cuisine.

· **Techniques**

Subsistence agriculture of the tropical humid regions of the Americas and Asia is based on the cultivation of gardens and is characterized by a multi-storey cropping system, made of mixed cropping and intercropping, with distinct canopy stratification (Fig. 3). These techniques are different from the ones used in

Fig. 4. Individual care provided to plants, Guadeloupe, 2000. Photo by the author.

Fig. 5. Dooryard garden surrounding the house and provision grounds in the background, Haiti 2000. Photo by the author.

the monocrop plantation fields and gardens of the temperate climate. Mixed cropping refers to the planting of multi-species crops while intercropping refers to the insertion of rows of the same crop among a mix of other crops. Distinct canopy stratification describes a vertical hierarchy where higher trees shelter smaller trees, crops and roots. These patterns of cultivation maximize sunlight, soil nutrients, and moisture to achieve the development of a greater number of species of plants in a given space. Gardens using these techniques are made of dozens, even hundreds of different vegetal species each represented by a small number of specimens that for many species require individual care to be planted and harvested (Fig. 4). The importance of the yield and the diversity of production is a contemporary topic of research for agronomists working in Caribbean humid tropical regions.[53]

The practice of slash-and-burn agriculture, as well as letting the land go fallow, were the usual ways to create a provision ground.[54] The origin of these practices is not known: it was taken for an Amerindian practice and perhaps a pan-tropical one at the time of the slave trade; however soon enough it was practiced by enslaved Africans and maroons.[55] Multi-storey cropping and canopy stratification were a striking characteristic of both provision grounds and dooryard gardens (Fig. 5).

When the provision grounds were located on the steep slopes of ravines, as in the volcanic island of Montserrat the use of erosion control strategies was necessary to retain the soil from washing away. The contour banking of soil was the technique used for this purpose. In her study of contemporary provision grounds of Montserrat, Lydia M. Pulshiper notes that the soil banks also present the advantage of providing the gardeners with stairways to work along the slopes. According to geographer Carl Sauer this technique of erosion control was learned from Amerindians at the beginning of the European colonization.[56]

The Definition of Subjectivity

Haitian *lakou* (from the French "La cour," referring to a kin-based and residential unit made of a cluster of houses and land property) and Jamaican yards are places that forged and were forged by kinship ties and this even before the abolition of slavery in the case of Jamaica.[57] Kinship ties were knitted between the living and the dead. In the Haitian context the *lakou* shelters the cult of the ancestors. The first inhabitant of the *lakou* is the protective spirit (*loa*) of the place and of the members of the family even when they migrate abroad. Haitian *lakou* and Jamaican yards are places that came to define family and collective identities.

Today, Guadeloupean dooryard gardens are places of ritual performances as diverse as planting the umbilical cords of the newborns at the bases of trees, sweeping the surroundings of the house in the morning, using labyrinthine paths to walk around the house and the garden, and protecting the dwelling against the spirits of the dead and sorcery attacks by adding protection on the walls of the house as well as planting specific plants and trees in precise locations in the yards. The accomplishment of these rituals led me to consider the dooryard gardens a kind of shell that mediates the inhabitants' relationships with their social and supernatural environments. Following Gaston Bachelard in his *Poetics of Space,* and Abraham A. Moles and Élisabeth Rohmer in their *Psychologie de l'espace,* the shells can be understood as the numerous protections laid on the body to link it to the environment or to protect it from outside elements.[58] These shells define the inhabitants' subjectivity through the practice of space.

Similar practices of space have been described elsewhere in the black diaspora. The practice of planting the umbilical cord at the base of trees and burying the placenta has been observed in Jamaica as well.[59] In Haiti and Jamaica a family cemetery located in yards seals definitively the links between the living and the dead.[60] This suggests that the study of the practice of space in dooryard gardens could lead to a broader understanding of the role of space in the definition of subjectivity.

African-American yards in the United States have been interpreted as places of remembrance for ancestors and as places that honor the world of the dead.[61] Although the interpretations tend to be convincing in their attempt to provide a reading of landscapes, perceived until then in a purely negative way, as made of trash and recycled artifacts placed in what seems to be pure fantasy and disorder, the reader never hears the voice of the people who laid out these gardens. The seemingly similar aesthetic appearance of some African-American gardens and Caribbean gardens should lead to further ethnographic-based investigations to establish a comparative understanding of a phenomenology of dooryard gardens.

Folklore, and historical and archaeological sources suggest that the Caribbean continuity between the self, the cabins and the gardens in relation to the social environment and the world of the dead and deities could well have been characteristic of enslaved dwellings since the beginning of slavery. In the United States, numerous excavations of slave cabins or urban houses' quarters inhabited by slaves have revealed the presence of artifacts such as bottles, nails, shells, knives, forks, bags holding plant material, in recurrent places such as between walls of cabins, beneath hearths and sills, and northeastern corners of certain rooms. For a while these objects were considered to have been forgotten or dropped by their owner and recovered by chance during an excavation. More recently these assemblages have come to be read as material belonging to healers (the "healer kit" of the Jordan plantation, TX)[62] or, given the elements constituting these bundles and their location in the domestic space, they are analyzed as translating a worldview of African origin based on constant interactions between the living and their ancestors.[63] In the Caribbean, the excavation of the house-yard burials of enslaved Africans in Seville, Jamaica, has revealed the fundamental relation that links the self, the house and the gardens with the social environment and the world of the spirits of the dead.[64] Ethnographic research when combined with historical data suggests that this relationship existed. Richard Price has related how the earliest generations of enslaved Africans who escaped the plantations of today's Surinam and became the Saramaka maroons filled the American forests with deities and spirits when they created their gardens.[65] As they

Fig. 6. The development of Creole gardens in public housing, Guadeloupe 1999. Photo by the author.

were gardening, the maroons discovered an American landscape inhabited by forest spirits and deities whom they integrated into their own lineages. Richard Price does not rely upon the practices or representations of a specific ethnic group to trace the origins of the Saramaka way of gardening. In developing earlier theoretical positions he explains that these rituals of domestication of the American environment are the result of creolization processes based on intense inter-African syncretisms. Douglas Armstrong concurs that burial practices of enslaved Africans cannot be traced to any specific West African group or to "'whole' pan-African practices" but do "reflect generalized West-African influences," among them the house-yard burial complex.[66]

Conclusion

By drawing upon different disciplinary approaches this chapter has demonstrated how the experience of gardens contributed to the emergence and development of Creole cultures. Gardens originated in the plantations' landscapes and were characteristic of the rural regions of the Americas; however, they have not disappeared with the urbanization of these regions and the cramming together of people in buildings or the migrations of people to cities or other countries. Today gardens are emerging in three new contexts. First, gardens are created by the inhabitants of housing estates and public housing in recently urbanized rural regions. Plots of plants and trees emerge on the ground level of public housing buildings, and balconies of the same buildings become sites of miniaturized gardens (Fig. 6). Second, when Caribbean people migrate to cities or other countries, even to Brooklyn, NY, some of them do recreate gardens in their new settlements, either a dooryard garden or a balcony garden. The study of the experience that people have of their gardens when they relocate to a different environment (from a rural area to an urban one, from a house to an apartment) or society (from a Caribbean island to the United States or Europe) can open new research directions in the role of gardens in the development of identities and cultural forms. Finally, gardens are becoming emblematic of heritage politics. In Guadeloupe, gardens have been created as sites for the performances of an institutionalized folklore or as conservatories of horticultural traditions and botanical knowledge. In rural Haiti, gardens have been designed to promote medicinal plants. Several Jamaican and American archaeological gardens have become essential reconstructions in the representation of slavery. The discourse underlying these reconstructions has to be elucidated. Given these new contexts the study of gardens in the African diaspora is an emerging field and its future might lie in the study of gardens in urban context.

Bibliography

Armstrong, Douglas V. "African-Jamaican Housing at Seville: A Study in Spatial Transformation." *Archaeology Jamaica (New Series)* 6 (1992): 51-63.

Armstrong, Douglas and Mark L. Fleischman. "House-Yard Burials of Enslaved Laborers in Eighteenth-Century Jamaica." *International Journal of Historical Archaeology* 7 n°1 (2003): 33-65.

Armstrong, Douglas and Ken Kelly "Settlements Patterns and the Origins of African Jamaican Society: Seville Plantation, St. Anne's Bay, Jamaica." *Ethnohistory* 47 n°2 (2000): 369-397.

Bachelard, Gaston. *La poétique de l'espace.* Paris: PUF, 1957.

Barrau, Jacques, ed. *Etude comparative des facteurs socio-culturels relatifs à la santé et à l'environnement dans les petites Antilles*, Rapport CNRS, Action thématique programmée "Santé et environnement". Paris: Museum National d'Histoire Naturelle, 1986.

Beckford, William. *A Descriptive Account of the Island of Jamaica.* London: Printed for T. and J. Egerton, 1790.

Bennett, Harry J. *Bondsmen and Bishops - Slavery and Apprenticeship on the Codrington Plantations of Barbados, 1710-1838.* Berkeley: University of California Press, 1958.

Benoît, Catherine. *Corps, jardins, mémoires - Anthropologie du corps et de l'espace à la Guadeloupe.* Paris: Éditions de la Maison des sciences de l'homme/Éditions du CNRS, 2000.

Berlin, Ira, and Philip D. Morgan. *The Slaves' Economy: Independent Production by Slaves in the Americas.* London: Frank Cass, 1991.

Berlin, Ira, and Philip D. Morgan. *Cultivation and Culture: Labor and the Shaping of Slave Life in the Americas.* Charlottesville and London: University Press of Carolina, 1993.

Besson, Jean. *Martha Brae's Two Histories: European Expansion and Caribbean Culture-Building in Jamaica.* Chapel Hill & London: University of North Carolina Press, 2002.

Brown, Kenneth L. "Material Culture and Community Structure: The Slave and Tenant Community at Levi Jordan's Plantation, 1848-1892." *In Working toward Freedom: Slave Society and Domestic Economy in the American South,* edited by Larry E. Hudson Jr., 95-118. Rochester, NY: University of Rochester Press, 1994.

Carmichael, A. C. Mrs. *Domestic Manners and Social Condition of the White, Colored, and Negro Population of the West Indies.* London: Whittaker, Treacher, and Co, 1833.

Carney, Judith A. *Black Rice - The African Origins of Rice Cultivation in the Americas.* Cambridge, MA: Harvard University Press, 2001.

Casid, Jill H. *Sowing Empire: Landscape and Colonization.* Minneapolis, MN: University of Minnesota Press, 2005.

Certeau, Michel de. *The Practice of Everyday Life.* Berkeley, Los Angeles & London: University of California Press, 1984 transl. by Steven Randall from *L'invention du quotidien* [1980].

Chaplin, Joyce. *An Anxious Pursuit: Agricultural Innovation and Modernity in the Lower South, 1739-1815.* Chapel Hill, NC: University of Carolina Press, 2003.

Chivallon, Christine. *Espace et identité à la Martinique: Paysannerie des mornes et reconquête collective (1840-1860).* Paris: CNRS Éditions, 1998.

Coleridge, Henry N. *Six Months in the West Indies, in 1825.* New York: G. & C. Carvill, E. Bliss and E. White, 1826.

Conan, Michel. *Essais de poétique des jardins.* Firenze, Italy: Leo S. Olschki, 2004.

Curtin, Philip D. *The Rise and Fall of the Plantation System. Essays in Atlantic History.* Cambridge, MA: Cambridge University Press, 1990.

Cuvelier, Jean. *L'ancien Congo d'après les archives romaines,* Brussels, 1954.

Debien, Gabriel. "La nourriture des esclaves sur les plantations des Antilles françaises aux 17e et 18e siècles." *Caribbean Studies* 4 n°2 (1964): 3-27.

Degras, Lucien. *Le jardin créole, Repères culturels, scientifiques et techniques.* Guadeloupe: Éditions Jasor and Archipel des Sciences, 2005.

Delle, James A. *An Archaeology of Social Space: Analyzing Coffee Plantations in Jamaica's Blue Mountains.* New York and London: Plenum, 1998.

Dutton, Thomas A., and Lian H. Mann. *Reconstructing Architecture: Critical Discourses and Social Practices,* Minneapolis, MN: University of Minnesota Press, 1996.

Edwards, Bryan. *The History, Civil and Commercial of the British Colonies of the West Indies.* Dublin, 1793.

Edwards, Ywonne E. 'Trash revisited' - A Comparative Approach to Historical Descriptions and Archaeological Analysis of Slave Houses and Yards". In *Keep Your Head to the Sky - Interpreting African-American Ground,* edited by Grey Gundaker, 245-271. Charlotteville & London: University Press of Virginia, 1998.

Ferguson, Leland. *Uncommon Ground: Archaeology and Early African America, 1650-1800.* Washington, D.C.: Smithsonian Institution Press, 1992.

Fournet, Jacques. *Flore illustrée des phanérogammes de Guadeloupe et de Martinique.* Trinité, Martinique (FWI): Godwana Editions, 2002.

Gaspar, David B. "Slavery, Amelioration, and Sunday Markets in Antigua, 1823-1831." *Slavery and Abolition* 9 (1988): 1-26.

Gosse, Philip H. *A Naturalist's Sojourn in Jamaica.* London: Longman, Brown, Greean and Longmans, 1851.

Grant, Bradford C. "Accommodation and Resistance: The Built Environment and the African American Experience." In *Reconstructing Architecture: Critical Discourses and Social Practices,* edited by Thomas A. Dutton and Lian H. Mann, 202-233. Minneapolis, MN: University of Minnesota Press, 1996.

Grimé, William E. *Ethno-Botany of the Black Americans.* Algonac, MI: Reference Publications Inc, 1979.

Gundaker, Grey. "Tradition and Innovation in African-American Yards." *African Arts* XXVI n°2 (1993): 58-71.

Gundaker, Grey. "African-American History, Cosmology and the Moral Universe of Edward Houston's Yard." *Journal of Garden History* XIV n°3 (1994): 179-205.

Gundaker, Grey. "At Home on the Other Side: African American Burials as Commemorative Landscapes." In *Places of Commemoration: Search for Identity and Landscape Design,* edited by Joachim Wolschke-Bulmahn, 27-54. Washington, D.C.: Dumbarton Oaks, 2001.

Gundaker, Grey. "William Edmondson's Yard." In *The Art of William Edmondson,* edited by Robert F. Thompson, William Edmondson, Rusty Freeman, Lowery Stokes Sims, Judith McWillie, Bobby Lovett and Grey Gundaker, 61-70. Nashville, TN. & Jackson, MS, Cheekwood Museum of Art; University Press of Mississippi, 2000.

Gundaker, Grey *Keep Your Head to the Sky: Interpreting African American Home Ground.* Charlottesville, VA: University Press of Virginia, 1998.

Haagensen, Reimert, ed. and Arnold R. Highfield trans. *Beskrivelse over Eylander St. Croix i America i Vest-Indien - Description of the Island of St. Croix in America in the West Indies.* St. Croix, USVI: The Virgin Islands Humanities Council, 1994 [1758].

Haviser, Jay, ed. *African Sites Archaeology in the Caribbean.* Princeton, NJ and Kingston, Jamaica: Markus Wiener Publishers and Ian Randle Publishers, 1999.

Heath, Barbara J. "Bounded Yards and Fluid Boundaries: Landscapes of Slavery at Poplar Forest." In *Place of Cultural Memory: African Reflections on the American Landscape,* Conference Proceedings, 69-81. Washington, D.C.: Cultural Resources Diversity Program, Office of Diversity and Special Projects, National Park Service, 2001.

Heath, Barbara J., and Amber Bennett "'The little Spots allow'd them': The Archaeological Study of African-American Yards." *Historical Archaeology* 34 n°2 (2000): 38-55.

Higman, Barry W. "The Spatial Economy of Jamaican Sugar Plantations: Cartographic evidence of the Eighteenth and Nineteenth Centuries." *Journal of Historical Geography* 13 n° (1987): 17-19.

Higman, Barry W. *Jamaica Surveyed.* Barbados/Jamaica/Trinidad and Tobago: University of the West Indies Press, 1988.

Higman Barry W. *Montpelier, Jamaica : A Plantation Community in Slavery and Freedom 1739-1912.* Barbados, Jamaica, Trinidad & Tobago: The Press University of the West Indies, 1998.

Hudson Jr., Larry E. *Working toward Freedom: Slave Society and Domestic Economy in the American South.* Rochester, NY: University of Rochester Press, 1994.

Hunt, John Dixon, and Joachim Wolschke-Bulmahn. *Vernacular Gardens.* Washington, D.C.: Dumbarton Oaks, 1993.

Innis, Donald Q. *Intercropping and the Scientific Basis of Traditional Agriculture,* Intermediate Technology Development Group Publishing: UK, 1997.

Johnson, James. *N°1, 2, 3 of a Series of Views in the West Indies: Engraved from Drawings taken recently in the Islands: With letter press explanations made from actual observation.* London: Smith Elder, and Co. Cornhill for vol. 1 & 2, Underwood for vol. 3, 1827-1829.

Koster, Henry. "On the Amelioration of Slavery." In *The Pamphleteer* 8 n°76 (1816): 305-336.

Lewis, Matthew G. *Journal of a West-India Proprietor, Kept During a Residence in the Island of Jamaica.* London: J. Murray, 1834.

Marshall, Woodville K. "Provision ground and Plantation Labor in Four Windward Islands: Competition for Resources During Slavery." In *Cultivation and Culture: Labor and the Shaping of Slave Life in the Americas,* edited by Ira Berlin and Philip D. Morgan, 203-242. Charlottesville, VA and London: University Press of Carolina, 1993.

McDonald, Roderick A. "Independent Economic Production by Slaves on Antebellum Louisiana Sugar Plantations" In *The Slaves' Economy: Independent Production By Slaves in the Americas,* edited by Berlin, Ira and Philip D. Morgan, 182-208. London: Frank Cass, 1991.

McKee, Larry. "The Ideals and Realities Behind the Design and Use of 19th-Century Virginia Slave Cabins." In *The Art and Mystery of Historical Archaeology: Essays in Honor of James Deetz,* edited Anne Yentsch and Mary C. Beaudry, 195-213. Ann Arbor, MI: CRC Press, 1992.

Miller, Naomi F. and Kathryn L. Gleason. *The Archeology of Garden and Field,* Philadelphia, PA: University of Pennsylvania Press, 1994.

Mintz, Sidney W. *Caribbean Transformations.* New York and Oxford: Columbia University Press, 1974.

Mintz, Sidney W., and Douglas Hall. "The Origins of Jamaican Internal Marketing System." *Yale University Publications in Anthropology* 57: 3-26, 1960.

Moles, Abraham and Élisabeth Rohmer. *Psychologie de l'espace.* Tournai: Casterman, 1972.

Olwig, Karen F. *Cultural Adaptation and Resistance on St. John: Three Centuries of Afro-Caribbean Life.* Gainesville: University Presses of Florida, 1985.

Orser Jr., Charles E. "On Plantations and Patterns." *Historical Archaeology* 23 n°2 (1989): 28-40.

Orser Jr., Charles E. *Race and the Archaeology of Identity.* Salt Lake City, UT: The University of Utah Press, 2001.

Ponansky, Merrick. "Africanist Reflections on African-American Archaeology." In "*I, Too, Am America" Archaelogical Studies of African-American Life* edited by Theresa Sinngleton, 21-37. Charlottesville and London, University Press of Virginia, 1999.

Price, Richard. "On the Miracle of Creolization: A Retrospective." *New West Indian Guide* 75 n° 1/2 (2001): 35-64.

Price, Richard. "Africans Discover America: The Ritualization of Gardens, Landscapes, and Seascapes by Suriname Maroons." In *Sacred Rituals in Gardens and Landscapes,* edited by Michel Conan. Washington, D.C.: Dumbarton Oaks, (forthcoming).

Price, Richard, and Sally Price. *John Gabriel Stedman's Narrative of a Five Years Expedition Against the Revolted Negroes of Surinam In Guiana on the Wild Coast of South-America from the year 1772 to the year 1777.* Baltimore, MD: The Johns Hopkins University Press, 1988.

Pulsipher, Lydia M. "They have Saturdays and Sundays to Feed Themselves: Slave Gardens in the Caribbean." *Expedition* 32 n° 2 (1990): 24-33.

Pulsipher, Lydia M. "The Landscapes and Ideational Roles of Caribbean Slave Gardens." *In The Archeology of Garden and Field,* edited by Naomi F. Miller and Kathryn L. Gleason, 202-221. Philadelphia, PA: University of Pennsylvania Press, 1994.

Pulsipher, Lydia M., and LaVerne Wells-Bowie. "The Domestic Spaces of Daufuskie and Monserrat: A Cross-Cultural Comparison." *Cross-Cultural Studies of Traditional Dwelling* 7 (1989): 1-28.

Pérez de la Riva, Francisco. *La Habitación Rural en Cuba.* La Habana: Contribución del Grupo Guamá, Anthropologia, 26, 1952.

Ramusio, Giovanni Battista. *Navigazioni e viaggi.* Torino: G. Einaudi, 1978.

Ruppel, Timothy, Jessica Neuwirth, Mark P. Leone, and Gladys-Marie Fry. "Hidden in View: African Spiritual Spaces in North American Landscapes." *Antiquity* (June 2003): 343-359.

Sauer, Carl O. "Economic Prospects of the Caribbean". In *The Caribbean: Its Economy,* edited by Alva C. Wilgus, 15-27. Gainesville, FL: University of Florida Press, 1954.

Schlotterbeck, Robert T. "The Internal Economy of Slavery in Rural Piedmont Virginia." *In Cultivation and Culture: Labor and the Shaping of Slave Life in the Americas,* edited by Ira Berlin and Philip D. Morgan, 170-181. Charlottesville, VA and London: University Press of Carolina, 1993.

Schwartz, Stuart B. *Slaves, Peasants, and Rebels: Reconsidering Brazilian Slavery,* Urbana, IL: University of Illinois, 1992.

Singleton, Theresa A., ed. *'I, Too, Am America' Archaeological Studies of African-American Life.* Charlottesville, VA and London: University Press of Virginia, 1999.

Singleton, Theresa A., and Mark D. Bograd, eds. *The Archaeology of the African Diaspora in the Americas.* Ann Arbor, MI: Braun-Brumfield, 1995

St. George, Robert B. *Material Life in America 1600-1860.* Boston, MS: Northeastern University Press, 1988.

Thompson, Robert F. *Flash of the Spirit: African and Afro-American Art and Philosophy.* New York, NY: Vintage Books, 1983.

Thompson, Robert F. "Bighearted Power - Kongo Presence in the Landscape and Art of Black America." In *Keep Your Head to the Sky - Interpreting African-American Ground,* edited by Grey Gundaker, 38-92. Charlottesville, VA and London, University Press of Virginia, 1998.

Thompson, Robert F. "Edmondson's Art." In *The Art of William Edmondson,* edited by Robert F. Thompson, William Edmondson, Rusty Freeman, Lowery Stokes Sims, Judith McWillie, Bobby Lovett and Grey Gundaker, 3-14. Nashville, TN and Jackson, MS, Cheekwood Museum of Art: University Press of Mississippi, 2000.

Thornton, John. *Africa and Africans in the Making of the Atlantic World, 1400-1680.* Cambridge, UK: Cambridge University Press, 1992.

Tobin, Beth F. *Colonizing Nature: The Tropics in British Arts and Letters, 1760-1820.* Philadelphia, PA: University of Pennsylvania Press, 2005.

Tomich, Dale. *Slavery in the Circuit of Sugar: Martinique in the World Economy, 1830-1848.* Baltimore, MD: Johns Hopkins University Press, 1990.

Tomich, Dale. "Une petite Guinée: Provision Ground and Plantation in Martinique, 1830-1848." In *The Slaves' Economy: Independent Production by Slaves in the Americas,* edited by Ira Berlin and Philip D. Morgan, 68-91. London: Frank Cass, 1991.

Trollope, Anthony. *The West Indies and the Spanish Main.* London: Chapman & Hall, 1860.

Trouillot, Michel-Rolph. *Peasants and Capital.* Baltimore, MD and London: The Johns Hopkins University Press, 1988.

Westmacott, Richard N. "Pattern and Practice in Traditional African-American Gardens in Rural Georgia." *Landscape Journal* 10 n°2 (1991): 87-104.

Westmacott, Richard N. *African-American Gardens and Yards in the Rural South.* Knoxville, TN: University of Tennessee Press, 1992.

Westmacott, Richard N. "The Gardens of African-Americans in the Rural South." In *Vernacular Gardens* edited by John Dixon Hunt, and Joachim Wolschke-Bulmahn, 77-104. Washington, D.C.: Dumbarton Oaks, 1993.

Westmacott, Richard N. "Gardening, Yard Decoration, and Agriculture Among Peoples of African Descent in the Rural South and in the Cayman Islands." In *In Place of Cultural Memory: African Reflections on the American Landscape,* Conference Proceedings, 135-138. Washington, DC: Cultural Resources Diversity Program, Office of Diversity and Special Projects, National Park Service, 2001.

Wilgus, Alva C. *The Caribbean: Its Economy.* Gainesville, FL: University of Florida Press, 1954.

Wolschke-Bulmahn, Joachim. *Places of Commemoration: Search for Identity and Landscape Design.* Washington, D.C.: Dumbarton Oaks, 2001.

Yentsch, Anne E. and Mary C. Beaudry. *The Art and Mystery of Historical Archaeology: Essays in Honor of James Deetz.* Ann Arbor, MI: CRC Press, 1992.

Notes

[1] This essay is based on library research that I accomplished as a fellow in the Garden and Landscape Studies at Dumbarton Oaks in 2000-2001 and in the summer of 2003, and as an associate researcher at the Gilder Lehrman Center at Yale University in the fall of 2004. I would like to thank Mark Zapatka and Bridget Gazzo at Dumbarton Oaks who tirelessly managed to get all the documents that I requested during my two residencies. Thanks to a Wenner-Gren foundation individual research grant (2001) I was able to visit some archaeological excavations of plantation slave quarters in the Caribbean and the U.S. This fieldwork complemented the written records but also gave me a sense of the diversity of space plantation contexts which informs the argument of this chapter.

[2] Trollope 1860, 28.

[3] Casid 2005, Tobin 2005

[4] Johnson, 1827-1829, vol. 1, 8.

[5] Marshall 1993.

[6] Haagensen and Highfield (1758) [1994], 23.

[7] Schlotterbeck 1993, 174.

[8] Lewis 1834, 85 in Higman 1988, 263.

[9] (Marshall 1993, 50-51.

[10] "Palinkas" comes from "palenques" which refers to maroon settlements.

[11] For an understanding of gardens from this perspective see Conan 2004.

[12] In the case of Martinique preceding the abolition of slavery see Tomich 1991, 77.

[13] In an interview conducted in the 1940s, under the auspices of the Slave Narrative Collection of the Federal Writers' Project, Elizabeth Ross Hite remembers that she and her fellow slaves "had a garden right in front of our quarter. We planted ev'rything in it. Had watermelon, mushmelon, and a flower garden" in (McDonald 1991, 186)

[14] In Jamaica in the first half of the 19th century (Higman 1988, 252-256).

[15] Heath and Bennett 2000, 38.

[16] Pulsipher 1994, 202-221.

[17] Although in Jamaica at the beginning of European colonization they were located close to the sugar mills where water was available (Edwards 1793).

[18] Slaves in St. John had commercial relations with slaves in St. Thomas. See (Olwig 1985, 45).

[19] Pérez de la Riva 1952 in Mintz 1974, 237.

[20] Gaspar 1988

[21] Mintz 1974.

[22] For a presentation of the current debates about the slave economy see Berlin and Morgan (1991 and 1993).

[23] For a synthesis of this research see (Degras 2005).

[24] Gundaker 1993, 1994, 1998, 2000, 2001; Heath 2000, 2001; Thompson 1983,1998, 2000; Westmacott 1991, 1992, 1993, 2001.

[25] Curtin 1990, Greenfield 1997.

[26] Thornton 1992, 170.

[27] Thornton 1992, 170.

[28] Thornton 1992, 174.

[29] Debien 1964.

[30] Berlin and Morgan 1991.

[31] Schwartz 1992.

[32] Bennett 1958.

[33] For Guadeloupe Benoît (2000), for Martinique (Tomich 1990), and for Saint-Domingue (Debien 1964).

[34] Coleridge 1826, 125-126.

[35] Certeau 1984.

[36] Pulsipher and Wells-Bowie 1989.

[37] Tomich 1991, 81.

[38] Delle 1998.

[39] Trouillot 1988 for Dominica and (Chivallon 1998) for Martinique have also demonstrated how peasant communities were formed after Emancipation through the purchase of former provision grounds.

[40] Fieldwork in Louisiana, February 2003.

[41] See the analysis of the excavation of the 18th century Seville plantation's slave quarters on the Northern coast of Jamaica (Armstrong 1992, Armstrong and Kelly 2000).

[42] Higman 1987, 1988.

[43] For the major role of enslaved Africans in the construction of the plantation buildings both for the slave quarters and the Great House, see (Grant 1996).

[44] McKee 1992.

[45] For a discussion about the role of the root cellars see (Ferguson 1992, Singleton 1995, Edwards 1998).

[46] Fournet, J. (2002).

[47] See the pioneering work of W. E. Grimé (Grimé 1979).

[48] The expression comes from J. A. Carney (Carney 2001, 156).

[49] This expression, which emphasizes the diversity of the flora, is from J. Barrau (Barrau 1986).

[50] Ponansky 1999.

[51] Chaplin 1993.

[52] Barbara Heath bases her interpretation of possible medicinal uses of plants found in the slave quarters of Poplar Forest on the uses described for these very same plants in Jefferson's Garden book (Heath 2001, 77).

[53] Degras 2005, Innis 1997.

[54] Gosse 1851.

[55] For Jamaica (Beckford 1790, Higman 1988, Mintz and Hall 1960), St. John (Olwig 1985) and the maroons of Surinam (Price and Price 1988).

[56] Sauer 1954 in Pulsipher 1990, 31.

[57] For a recent discussion of the lakou unit see J. M. Smith Smith (2002). For the description of extended family households organized as yards in the beginning of the 19th century in Jamaica see Higman (Higman 1998) and see J. Besson for the concept of family land (Besson 2002).

[58] Bachelard 1957, Moles and Rohmer 1972.

[59] Mintz 1974, 246.

[60] Besson 2002.

[61] See R. F. Thompson (Thompson 1983, 103–159 and 1998, 2000) and his student G. Gundaker (Gundaker 1993, 1994, 1998, 2000).

[62] Brown 1994.

[63] Ruppel, Neuwirth, Leone, and Fry 2003.

[64] Armstrong and Fleischman 2003.

[65] Price, forthcoming.

[66] Armstrong and Fleischman 2003, 40.

Gardens and Cultural Change: A Pan-American Perspective

Gardens and Cultural Change: A Pan-American Perspective

Gardens and Cultural Change: A Pan-American Perspective

Gardens and Cultural Change: A Pan-American Perspective

An Ideological-Aesthetic Approach to Buenos Aires Public Parks and Plazas

Sonia Berjman

Introduction

What makes the public promenade a vital urban element are the ways it reflects the rise of power, the colonization of ideas, the economical status of a country, the population's educational level, urban hygienic achievements, governmental policies, distinctions between social segments, evolution of art and science and, above all, society's ideological scenery. Buenos Aires' public promenades clearly validate this point. The city was founded in 1580 in the style of and with the same purposes as all Spanish cities in the New World: to impose land and space domination, population hierarchy, and diversified uses. But during the next four centuries it developed in other directions. Its major square, church atria, neighborhood squares, poplar grove, its market squares, and parks, were born in one way but then were shaped by the different factors just listed.

What were our relations with the prestigious metropolis, with the broadening centers of modernity? Did we copy, did we import, did we appropriate? Which were the causes and the effects? Which were the physical and symbolic results? Which were the different turning points, the resulting urban artifacts, the changing social performances, the urban plans, the different political practices? Who were the social actors involved: citizens, landscapers, mayors?

Public promenades have a dynamic life as they are the result of the whole environmental situation. They must be studied as a net, never as a thread. They are complex artifacts which help us to understand different populations and cultures. The relationship between their physical aspects (shapes, vegetation, furniture, locations and urban space management) and their intangible facets (uses, appropriations and social practices and meanings) derives from their ideological birth and evolution.

Power struggles, prestigious models, outstanding *entrepreneurs*, social needs and achievements, urban policies, changing political situations are all extremely appealing approaches to the unique character of a public structure. In this sense, social needs often become social issues when transforming elite spaces into democratic spaces for recreation or other social demands. Buenos Aires' civic plazas as well as urban parks and neighborhood squares experienced those changes both in their physical shape and in their social function and significance.

Can We Talk About an American Southern Cone Way?

The absence of a significant indigenous heritage and the genocide of both the Aboriginal population and the Negro slaves influenced the construction of Buenos Aires as a city conceived by Europeans entirely for Europeans, but on American soil.

It is useful to point out that most Latin-American promenades (from Mexico to Argentina) followed the same pattern as Buenos Aires' ones. Certainly that was the case of the American Southern Cone. This paper will present a case study that explains the evolution of a certain type of public space in this entire region—Chile, Argentina, Uruguay, and South Brazil—as our general development followed the same outlines.

For us, Southern Latin-Americans, the word "America" does not mean the United States of America only, but refers to our entire continent, from Alaska to Patagonia. In the same sense, we identify ourselves as Americans. I am conscious that historical research implies a first contextual clipping colored by the researcher's ideology, as Marina Waisman, pioneer in Latin American urban history, taught us so many years ago. I can speak from my cultural identity perspective.[1] As Ortega y Gasset *dixit*: from the human being and his circumstance.

I also want to state that we face a linguistic problem, since Spanish is a language with a vast vocabulary and sometimes it becomes difficult to translate properly our own made-up concepts into English.

Moreover, we, Southern Cone Latin Americans, neither consider ourselves anthropological objects of study, nor exotic examples for export. We do not feel as the rest of Latin Americans or as real Europeans. We neither feel like *gauchos* (local cowboys), nor *tango* fans, nor again as transmigrated Parisians. We have our own deep and lasting inconsistencies.

A Beginning That Lasted Three Centuries (1580-1880)

Buenos Aires was founded for its second time in 1580, and this foundation gave birth to the big, heterogeneous, crowded but beautiful and generally European city of today.[2]

Spanish urbanism was the first foreign influence to reach our region. Their *plaza*, or "square," element was of great importance (Berjman 2001). The Spanish conquerors found in indigenous America several public spaces like European ones, although of different physical shape. In the indigenous world, those urban public spaces were either huge scenes located on the two principal urban axes, or markets—open air spaces located here and there. Those plazas—the first for religious and/or political ceremonies and the second for commerce and social encounters—showed the power of different groups, distinguished by their location and use. They had no vegetation but wide areas where crowds could gather. Gardening was reserved to private gardens, which were imaginative and luxurious, due to the variegated local flora and to the high standard of civilization. This situation prevailed from Mexico down to Peru, but not to the Southern Cone where indigenous communities did not achieve such a cultural level. But, in any case, it is an important heritage that Spanish founders could not overlook.

The Spanish plaza's origin must be traced to the Middle Ages. It was the result of the Christian and Muslim cultures creating one integrated, improved, conceptualized product ready for export to the conquered America: the market-square. In Spain, it was born little by little when, during the eleventh century, beyond the city walls markets began to be placed in market buildings and the vacant spaces became urban neighbors' plazas as we know them today. The development of the geometrical and methodical Renaissance city in the fourteenth and fifteenth centuries gravely changed those ancient Spanish-Muslim settlements. The *nova urbe* concept—with its wider and straight streets, regular squares, its open perspectives and its promenades—was literally built over the old Mohammedan cities.

The ideal Renaissance city had a huge central space or square, with the principal building set apart on the axis, the church being the usual focal point, and all entrances to the square having the same importance. Some of Vitruvio's or Alberti's classical treatises' rules were exactly repeated in the *Leyes de Indias* ("Laws of the Indias"), Spanish Settlement Regulations given by Philip II in 1573, which every founder had to follow strictly. (Also, as major indigenous American cultures did, Muslim Spain reserved gardens for private enjoyment.)

Fig. 1. The Plaza Mayor during a civic commemoration, 1844, Isola's painting. Argentinean National Archives.

The Plaza Mayor (Major Square)

These regulations established the choice of city site by a riverside, the orthogonal and geometrical grid, the exact location of the most important buildings, and the major and minor squares to be built in the new city. This original shaping factor determined, first of all, the enactment of the city's foundation in the space destined to be the Plaza Mayor. Hence this orientation point in the embryonic city assigned place to the most important functions of the time: justice (the gallows stood in its center), religion (the main Catholic church faced the Plaza), militia barracks and administration (both buildings stood on the other side of the Plaza). The Plaza Mayor represented the idea of the conquest, the presence of a hierarchical order that had to be respected and submitted to.

Nevertheless, the capital meaning of the Plaza Mayor was as "the" social space for everybody. The main open-air city market took place there, where Indians, Spaniards and *Criollos* (born in the New World) sold and bought all kinds of goods. It was the rejoicing space wherein occurred games, jousts, bull fights, sports, masked balls, the publication of royal edicts, Saints' and Emperors' feasts, military triumph celebrations and/or Catholic processions. This was where the "lady" could meet the "negro slave"—one buying, the other going to the river to laundry; where the soldiers and the priests could pass each other while walking to their respective jobs, and where all enjoyed bull fights—the truly egalitarian encounter.

Rectangular in contour, it was huge, wide, dusty in summer and muddy in winter (since unpaved), continuously changing its appearance by means of an ephemeral architecture of stands, boxes, palisades, platforms, triumphal arches, which served for all sorts of human entertainment.

Buenos Aires' Plaza Mayor—today *Plaza de Mayo*—exceeded the deep significance of the Conquest's political-economical-Christianizing character, to achieve a symbolic value enhanced by the addition of multiple functions and their

Fig. 2. The Alameda or Poplar Grove, Isola's drawing, c. 1840. Argentinean National Archives.

meanings. (Gutiérrez and Hardoy 1985) (Fig. 1). As centuries passed by, this inner and hidden symbolism developed into a more physical signification and the Plaza Mayor became the most powerful political space of the country, or, as we say, Argentina's heart. Briefly, the one who achieves the "possession" of this space— even momentarily, with its occupation by thousands of people manifesting their loyalty— assumes real power, independent of his status as person, group, government, population, establishment or outsider.

Other Plazas and Promenades

In addition to the Plaza Mayor, several *huecos* (literally "holes," or smaller plazas) occupied empty lots located in different neighborhoods and served as local markets or specialized markets (wine, leather, grains, etc.). Church porches and atria served for social encounters before or after the masses in a totally religious society (even time was known by the bell's playing summons to masses). *Plazuelas* (little plazas) adjacent to churches and convents were used for musical and theatre purposes (Berjman 2001).

The *Alameda* (poplar grove)—the first promenade to be thought as a recreational space, in 1757—was a short avenue parallel to the Plata River planted with willows (as we did not have poplars!). It followed the Sevilian pattern that had been developed all over Hispanic America. The changes in the ways of life experienced during the eighteenth century gave birth to these specific spaces "for soul relaxation during the moments given to restoration" as Peruvian Viceroy Amat said circa 1770.[3] In Buenos Aires, it was the desire to create a "sheltered atmosphere for those who promenade by feet, by horse or by carriage." (Rípodas Ardanaz no data). From the very first moment, it became the democratic promenade, where everybody went to profit from its privileged situation by the river shore, on the edge of the cliff. As it was located close to the port, it became the respectful image given to the visitors by a city that desired to grow to higher standards (Fig. 2).

It was not until the beginning of the nineteenth century that built-on-purpose bullrings appeared in Buenos Aires. At this time, the city's population began to divide itself into different social classes, each one with its own living and recreational habits. It was then that amusement architecture was born providing adequate buildings for cock fights, bull fights, and theatre performances. Nevertheless, all those actions continued taking place in traditional public spaces—where they were originally born—but they had a short life as animal spectacles were soon prohibited by the 1813 Assembly, which also banned slavery among other matters.

This was, in a general scheme, the public open space grid (in addition to streets) of colonial Buenos Aires and other Argentinean cities, from Spanish foundation and conquest to late Organization time (1880). The Spanish scheme permanently shaped the future of the city, since a structure of this kind cannot be changed through urban development. So, it was over this grid-scheme that the French model came to stay until today, together with a few bizarre examples of the Dictatorship's model.

The "Modernization" Following Paris Lights (1880-1950)

It was in the middle of the nineteenth century that the Direction des Promenades de Paris was organized under the direction of French landscaper Adolphe Alphand. He was committed to effectualize the Baron de Haussmann's plan of city modernization. In this plan, green public spaces had a very strong importance, and Paris was completely changed by opening streets, wide avenues and boulevards, by placing new squares in almost all neighborhoods, and by erecting enormous city parks throughout the four cardinal points of Paris (Jarrasé 1982). This new conception of the city (Vernes 1982)—in part brought by Napoleon III from London—was intended to replace an unhealthy and medieval city that was not easily managed, where dust, trash and lack of light were the common features in the streets and whose population was increasingly protesting the bad everyday living conditions. The result was that a new city model was accomplished for good, both for the government (since then the royal troops could quickly arrive to repress the usual social protests) and for the inhabitants (some recreational promenades improved the terrible and hard industrial working conditions).

This French Haussmann's urban model was promptly exported by the Paris city government to all the "civilized world" of the moment with the purpose to "civilize" it even more. Alphand knew that he was not only changing France's capital city but producing the basis of a conceptual change all over the world. He stated that his writings included technical advice "to those municipal administrations prepared to follow Paris's example from far away." He expected that Paris's changes "would encourage other city governments to follow that example and to establish several promenades [but] in the most modest proportions." In this way, the place of models and copies has been clearly established: in scale, in technology and in needs (real or affected). "… European horticulture achieved a world wide expansion through his calm conquest. That expansion has been done in all latitudes." Alphand reported (Alphand and Ernouf 1875).

Alphand's books on Paris promenades were sent all over the world, to libraries, authorities and wealthy citizens (both *L'art des jardins* and *Les promenades de Paris*). Buenos Aires, of course, was not excluded. During the second half of the nineteenth century the French urban model arrived in many different ways: books, newspapers, magazines, travelers. On the other hand, Argentinean aristocratic leaders, mayors, powerful business men, intellectuals and curious professionals traveled to Europe – but especially to Paris – to learn about this new and sophisticated "enlightening" city.

During the nineteenth century, Paris was the center of international culture, the site where one had to be, or to have been. This was the case of a young Argentinean painter, member of a gentry family, who studied at the École Polytechnique and became an engineer in the early 1850's, coming back to Buenos Aires at the time when its township government was organized (1854). Prilidiano Pueyrredon had remarkable skills as a technician and as an artist and was engaged by the local authorities to recycle our Plaza Mayor as the first accomplishment of an urban change.

His project included the embellishment of our unique monument at the time (the Independence Pyramid), pavement, benches, *parterres* and 300 trees planted geometrically all around the rectangular space. A chain over short columns encircled the square allowing only pedestrians to enter the new hierarchical space forbidden from that moment on to cattle, vehicles, merchants and other disturbing elements (Fig. 3).

Fig. 3. The Plaza Mayor with first French landscaping, Pueyrredon's drawing, 1856. Buenos Aires City Government Archives.
Fig. 4. Legend in the blackboard: Paris is the Capital of the civilized world, c. 1910. Argentinean National Archives.

When this remodeling was finished it deeply impressed the *porteños* (so called Buenos Aires inhabitants: people who live in a port city) and all neighbors wanted to have a similar although smaller plaza. During the following twenty-five years some three or four old plazas were "modeled" like the Plaza Mayor, as a shy beginning to impose the French model in place of the old Spanish model.

All those changes were attractive to a population that had begun to change importantly since Colonial times. At this moment, indigenous and African slaves began to diminish in number and European immigration began to replace them. This process continued with great emphasis, climaxing at the time of the celebration of the first Independence Centennial in 1910. At this point foreign population in Buenos Aires city reached fifty percent of the total population. In fact, population was divided equally between long-standing immigrant families and first-generation immigrants (Fig. 4).

The First Public Park[4]

At the beginning of the 1870's, President Domingo Faustino Sarmiento developed the idea of a city park for Buenos Aires, as a pastiche of developed countries' great parks, adapted to our city. He was influenced by the new nineteenth century European and North American urbanism but also by the thoughts of Argentinean physicians who followed the new ideas of urban "hygiene."

Sarmiento was a follower of the eighteenth century French Encyclopedia Movement, and his first book—written in 1845—had the very illuminating title of *Civilization and Barbarism*, presumably taken from Guillaume Thomas Raynal, whom he names. It was translated into French and published in Paris in 1853, and an English translation was published in the United States in 1868, showing an extraordinary First-World interest in his thought. To Sarmiento, cultivating land was a way to cultivate minds at the same time. He saw the deep split in our population (cultivated vs. uncultivated) and worked all his life to solve this gap. He was the founder of the Argentinean public school system by importing U.S. American teachers.[5]

During his 1867 visit to Paris he met Edouard André at the International Exhibition. André was 28 years old at that time and was building Sefton Park in Liverpool. He accompanied Sarmiento to visit Paris glass houses and other horticultural showcases. Sarmiento soon asked André to design a park system for Buenos Aires but–although he did it–unhappily it was not carried out[6] (Berjman 1998).

For Sarmiento, a park was "an equalitarian school:" "Among Buenos Aires' surprising developments (...) a park like the Bois de Boulogne, and Hyde Park or the Central Park of New York is missing. They offer exercise and natural beauties, art and daily enjoyment, as well as healthy sports not only to upper classes and foreigners but also to millions of artisans and their families" (Sarmiento 1874).

After several years of hard fights to convince Buenos Aires society and politicians of the use and healthy influence of a city park, Palermo Park (legally named Parque 3 de Febrero or February 3rd Park) was inaugurated in 1875. It was our first public park and it still holds a leading position among Argentinean public parks, although it has lost some of its original magnificence and a large proportion of its public land has gone into private hands. The first Palermo Park project was an international one. Technicians, landscapers, engineers, botanists, and horticulturists from France, Poland, Switzerland and Prussia gathered to achieve a high international standard, both scientific and aesthetic (Fig. 5).

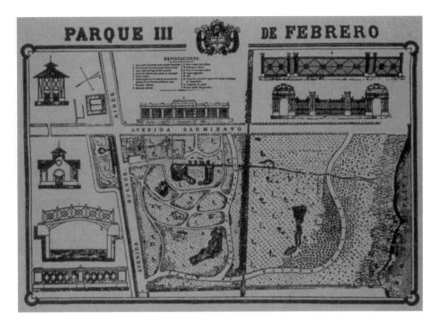

Fig. 5. The first Palermo Park project, 1875. Buenos Aires City Government Archives.

Fig. 6. Rocailles and grottos in Buenos Aires public promenades c. 1885. Argentinean National Archives.

Buenos Aires Capital City

The year 1880 marked a turning point in our history: Buenos Aires was declared National Capital by law. From 1880 to 1887 its population grew from 300,000 to 450,000 persons and city land increased from 4,400 hectares to 18,100 hectares as new borders were established. The Southern Great Capital began to turn from dream to fact. A legendary man was appointed as City

Fig. 7. Plaza de Mayo with Thays' landscaping, 1894. Argentinean National Archives.

Fig. 8. Paris images in Buenos Aires Palermo Park, della Valle painting, 1910. Buenos Aires City Government Archives.

Mayor: Torcuato de Alvear. His knowledge of Europe (he was a "frequent traveler" to the principal European cities and knew their mayors in person, Haussmann and others), and his determination to transform Buenos Aires into an outstanding South American city, led to the slogan "Buenos Aires as the Paris at the Plata River." It was a time of great change: from the old Spanish village to the new and modern "enlightened" French city, from the old Plaza Mayor and paved market squares to the new green *parterres*, topiary trees, Du Val d'Osne ornamental fountains, and huge urban parks. To promptly and successfully accomplish this goal, Mr. Alvear conceived and materialized a Haussmann like plan for Buenos Aires, in which open green spaces had uppermost importance.

Eugène Courtois was put in charge of promenades and parks.[7] He was a French gardener with wide experience and he transformed the old Spanish promenades (without vegetation) into French ones (with vegetation); he remodeled, built and created for ten years as Alphand had done in Paris. When Alvear and Courtois left the city administration, new teams arrived both in Paris and in Buenos Aires. The changes left were deep enough to be distinguished as "BTA" and "ATA": before Torcuato de Alvear and after Torcuato de Alvear, like B.C. and A.D. (Fig. 6).

Edouard André was appointed as Director of Promenades of Paris and he asked his principal assistant, Charles Thays, to come to Argentina for a years' work, but he stayed forever, hispanizing his name into Carlos Thays (Berjman 2002). He became "the Argentinean" landscaper, as he did not only change in quantity and quality Argentinean cities by planning and building around one hundred public promenades and one hundred private gardens and parks, but he also founded a dynasty-family of Argentinean landscapers that continue his work today. His enormous portfolio includes works in Uruguay, Chile and Brazil, the planning of our first National Parks (for nature preservation), the use of indigenous species, the introduction of garden-city urbanism, the creation of the modern Buenos Aires Botanical Garden, the issue of the first book on gardens, the reproduction of the *yerba mate* (national tea), the plantation of 100,000 trees in the streets, etc.

One of his first tasks as Promenades' Director was to contemporize the Plaza de Mayo, the ancient Plaza Mayor already transformed by Pueyrredon in the middle of that century. Thays asked if he had to "imitate the Place de la Concorde in Paris, eliminating the existing palm trees, or if he was expected to give it the same image as the other squares of the city." He concluded that "This work must be executed giving advantage to sane reasons against routine ideas" (Annual City Government Report 1890-92). The result was a combination of Place de la Concorde with existing palm trees that stands up to today (Fig. 7).

No doubt that his cherished oeuvre was Plaza Francia (France Square) inaugurated in 1910 with the French gift of a splendid monument in the center given for for our Independence Centennial. It was there that one of the largest crowds ever known in Buenos Aires gathered to commemorate Paris' Liberation in 1945, in spite of Argentina's government's "neutrality" in the Second World War (Perón decade).

Another outstanding Thays development was Palermo Park's enlargement and recycling project. He left us a real Bois de Boulogne Park thousands of miles away from Paris, in the Northern Buenos Aires area. His unusual landscaping skills and his extraordinary botanical and horticultural experience made possible the vegetation groups, the lakes, the pelouses, the sporting facilities, the Botanical Garden, and the Zoo. Of course this park offered the perfect scenery for aristocratic meetings: the exact copy of the Paris Flower Parade, musical events, horse and bike riding, lunches and dinners at the Lake Pavilion, and the car tours with the first motor vehicles introduced in the country (Fig. 8). But, the landscaper creates copies or imports models and then the population appropriates them. Although it was born as an open-air "living room" for high society, soon proletarian groups enjoyed its vegetation, its lakes and its paths. Immigrants began to celebrate national feasts, employees and workers gathered on Sundays, and even vagabonds took the park as their home. That's why the city government quickly bought (1894) an ancient family park situated on the south zone of the city and Thays remodeled it: Lezama Park, with its grilles and strict ruling (with a weekly schedule of opening hours for male or female assistance) was very useful for High Society … for several years!

And then … the story did not repeat again as a new fashion reached Argentina: holidays by the seaside. That's why the upper class founded a new city: Mar del Plata. This city was founded in 1874, contemporary to the Palermo Park construction but achieved its real importance during the early 1900's. Low classes had to resign themselves to old city parks now empty of aristocratic families. So, which was born first: the new parks or the new habits? Probably, simultaneously.

Following our Parisian love, Joseph Bouvard, Paris Director of Promenades, was engaged by the Buenos Aires Mayor in 1907 to design a park plan for the city. He was highly paid and stayed for six weeks. For the first time, some voices objected that we had trained Argentinean landscapers. Bouvard proposed two main subjects: a new vehicular system (comprising thirty two diagonal avenues, only two of which were built) and a new park system (featuring twenty individual projects, only seven of which were built)[8] (Berjman 1998). Undoubtedly, they were few results for so many expectations. As a popular magazine explained, Bouvard's engagement was possible because of "our special affection for French architects and for the superiority —without a bit of envy– that we all recognize in them" (Caras y Caretas 1907).

Fig. 9. Children's playgrounds due to Carrasco social thoughts, 1916. Buenos Aires City Government Archives.

Fig. 10. Thays son's copy of a French garden in Buenos Aires public space, c. 1935. Buenos Aires City Government Archives.

EL MUNDO — MARTES, MAYO 23 DE 1939

Transformando el Lugar en Bellos Jardines

ASPECTO QUE presentan los trabajos de formación de extensos y modernos jardines que se efectúan en los terrenos de la Avenida Alvear, a la altura de Tagle, que anteriormente ocupaba el estadio de River Plate

In 1914, Thays' Argentinean disciple Benito Carrasco succeeded him as Director of Promenades, to introduce the social point of view in the use of public parks and squares.

"Studying a city's public promenades is enough to learn about its advances" he said when he took over his position, adding "This office has a social aim to fulfill" (Berjman 1997). His thought was illuminated by a diffuse socialist utopia. He was Buenos Aires' Director of Promenades from 1914 to 1918. Carrasco was a follower of the French public landscape tradition in Latin America but—at the same time—he was an innovator about the ideological management of public promenades, undoubtedly influenced by visiting the United States of America around 1908. For him, city advances were based on the adherence to the new science of urbanism as well as on the democratization of green public space, opening its recreational, sportive, educational and cultural resources to the workers. Tennis courts, soccer fields and children's puppet theaters began to be seen in public parks. Students' and workers' weekend competitions changed the usual parks' users. Finally, Buenos Aires' public parks were planned and used by the majority of its population (Fig. 9).

From 1920 to 1946, Carlos León Thays (son) increased and maintained Buenos Aires promenades. He was fired from his position at the advent of Perón's government. Thays' son recaptured the French formal garden more deeply than it had ever been done before. He even reproduced exactly some French private parks in Buenos Aires public space (Fig. 10). French civilization still lived as "the one" all over the world, including Buenos Aires. French cuisine became a model for an enormous middle class, French couture was bought directly in Paris by the upper class, French was the first foreign language to be studied and almost everybody could add some French expressions in common conversations.[9]

Argentina, it was said, was the result of English technology, French culture and Italian labor. This threefold *entente* was so strong that the United States' influence had a long, hard fight to enter into Argentinean civilization. In the 1930's Argentineans saw "the image of France engraved in the occidental and cultivated world since the 18th Century Illustration as the quintessence of civilization (...) What caused our acceptance of the high concept that France has of herself? (...) France had a very important advantage. It seemed to offer its civilization to any foreigner wishing it. It was made available for everybody ..." (Hobsbawn 2003)

Fig. 11. Andalusian Court in Palermo Park, 1929. Photo Sonia Berjman.

That statement was written by an outstanding English historian, Eric Hobsbawn, but it could easily be signed by many Latin American thinkers. What was really amazing is that since 1910, a group of the local "intelligentsia" proposed a Renaissance of the Spanish origin, taking into account that those were our real roots. This notion has been quite widespread, and was very profitable in literature, architecture, music, sculpture, painting ... but not in gardening! This neo-Spanish revival left us just four private Sevilian style gardens in Buenos Aires city, the four of them of public use nowadays: Larreta's Palace (today's Spanish Art Museum), Noel Palace (today's Hispanic American Museum), Rojas' residence (today's Rojas' Museum), Yrurtia's residence (today's Yrurtia Museum). The only publicly derived one is the Andalusian Court of Palermo Park, donated by the Andalusian government but designed by Thays' son (Fig. 11).

In this French environment it was not strange that Buenos Aires Mayor Carlos Noel, who graduated in France himself, engaged the prestigious Jean Claude Nicolas Forestier in 1923. This time, opposition to his trip was huge and savage, but the Mayor played his cards in such a way that finally Forestier came. Some of Bouvard's features were repeated: high fees, three weeks of stay, enormous help given by Thays son (Forestier simply copied Thays son's Park Plan for Buenos Aires), almost nothing executed of his own proposals. But a luxurious and huge volume was published, and the myth was born that everything done afterwards was because of his advice.

The stylistic features used during this period of French enlightenment included perspectives with never ending axes; centralism achieved by hard elements both in main and in secondary layouts; constant symmetry even in apparently romantic (or English) designs; geometrical, irregular and mixed designs; strict subordination to the Spanish urban grid (with very few exceptions). The formal-shaping vocabulary did the same, including the following natural and cultural elements: pelouses with belvederes and balustrades, use of water, tree-lined avenues, small forests, flower beds, art masterpieces, engineering devices, architectural pieces, surrounding grilles, *rocaille* ornaments, caves and artificial ruins. Some of those elements had no more than two or three decades of life—such as rocailles that disappeared with the advent of the twentieth century—but most of them are still living, although not in a very good shape.

How We Lost All Ways

Fig. 12. Roberto Burle Marx's Plaza Perú, 1974, today demolished. Photo Marta Montero.
Fig. 13. "Cement squares" by the military dictatorship, 1976-1980. Photo Sonia Berjman.

During the second half of the twentieth century, Argentinean society changed quickly and deeply. The bourgeois Buenos Aires changed into the massive Buenos Aires. It became a city of contrasts, instability and anguish. Instead of overseas immigration we had inner movement and transmigration over land borders (Bolivia, Paraguay). As elites looked for new status, the new middle class became powerful as never before. Buenos Aires began to be characterized as a metropolis of quantification and massification (Romero 1976). The tidy image of a European city shown to the world in the Independence Centennial of 1910 started to evaporate. The population reached three million but the regional suburbanization pushed it to ten million. Skyscrapers vs. shanty towns; downtown vs. metropolitan sprawl; cars, weekend houses, television, cinemas and theatres vs. poverty, exclusion and unemployment; a city intensely segmented: this is the scenario of the late twentieth century Buenos Aires.

A crisis has enveloped our society, and of course our culture, since then. During the last decades the searchers of the *dernier cri* believed they had finally achieved "modernism." In fact, we had run after "the modernity" for a century but we did not realize that it was an illusion.

After Thays son's age, Buenos Aires public green spaces were never again the same. Little by little, due to lack of maintenance, loss of vegetation, bad design, corruption and bad management, the splendid ensemble of promenades we had achieved by the middle of the twentieth century was ruined. Since then we have lost the way (Fig. 12).

Dictatorship's "Heavy Hands"

In the 1970's, postmodernism caused city fragmentation. In addition, we lost the original city-citizen unity, in a process caused by military dictatorships similar to Lewis Mumford tyrant-polis. The physical city was wounded by a highway system. "Cement squares"—or as we call them *plazas secas*—were introduced as a materialization of the ideology that assaulted power. The new "landscapers" were translators of the dictator's aims: they thought their work "a new urban landscape (…) that will reorganize the future human habitat (…) in a prophetic way …" (Fevre no data) (Fig. 13).

The vague landscaping products of the postmodern dictatorship had no more vegetation and no more people but concrete columns that support nothing. "The tree is the worst enemy of a modern or future technological civilization (…) a tree has never been seen in a Flash Gordon city (…) and it appears that the city concept is opposite to the nature concept" (Waisman 1985). This critical statement of Marina Waisman seems to be the gospel of those to whom the idea of technical-scientific progress is overwhelmingly superior to the concept of the garden as Nature and Lost Paradise.

We should not forget that the out-standing characteristics of gardens are their permanent change and growth, their everlasting mutation, their brevity. On the other hand, manmade reinforced concrete tries to stay forever; its aim is immutability, eternal presence. That is why parks and squares are needed in the city: they bring dynamism to the stillness of the environment. Forestier made a distinction between the *terre vivante* (city spaces for vegetation) and the *terre morte* (city spaces for vehicle parking). Those prophetic words show us the paradox inherent in the term "concrete square."

But, as we know, promenades change

Fig. 14. Madres' white handkerchiefs on Plaza de Mayo pavement, today. Photo Sonia Berjman.
Fig. 15. Floralis: stainless steel flower, today. Photo Sonia Berjman.

with the society that holds them. And during the military dictatorship the only people who defied power using a public square were the *Madres de Plaza de Mayo*. The ancient Plaza Mayor was the space chosen by the mothers of the *desaparecidos* (people who used to "disappear" or to "vanish" in military hands, but were really killed and their remains hidden or tossed in the river) to protest, to beg, to claim, to demand and to show themselves. And, as already suggested, physical changes accompany society's changes, or vice versa: big white handkerchiefs (similar to those that Mothers wear on their heads) have been painted on the ground, tracing the path where the Mothers weekly walk until today, although the Plaza Mayor is a Historical Landmark. For more than a quarter of a century, every Thursday at noon we all have an honor date: to accompany those old ladies in their turn

Fig. 16. Homeless people living in a plaza, today. Photo Sonia Berjman.
Fig. 17. French heritage still remaining in Buenos Aires. Photo Sonia Berjman.

around the Independence Pyramid in silence, in remembrance of the thousands of murdered and tortured (Fig. 14).

Democracy Finally Returns

From 1983 on, the return of democracy brought citizens again to the public space. Parks and squares were revisited, political parades returned to the Plaza de Mayo, community squares were born in different quarters. But corruption reappeared, bad administrations continued, there was no more money for public green spaces, and "godfathers" (private companies) were called to maintain such spaces —producing more corruption since they got advertising benefits as tutors of the most central and well placed promenades. The rest got little or no maintenance.

Several initiatives of the city government ended in promenades without aesthetic unity, without style and even without correct use and pleasure. Most conspicuous is a giant stainless steel mechanical flower that opens during mornings and shuts evenings, in a highly expensive procedure, occupying an ancient open *pelouse* where people used to spend sunny times, nowadays encircled with bars (Fig. 15).

Today, Buenos Aires has lost its "Paris Lights." Our beaux-arts urban, architectural and landscape heritage, including parks and squares, is in great danger. Little by little, homeless people are building shanty towns in certain parks, our urban tree-lined streets are losing their old splendor due to lack of replanting, art masterpieces are damaged by vandalism or stolen, original vegetation has been changed, and no one cares for designs (Fig. 16).

We do not see anything positive on the horizon; we are walking towards a Dark Age.

Conclusions

The urban shape of current Buenos Aires is the result of a four-century process, including successes and failures, improvements and back steps, projects and materializations, by both government and community. Public green spaces specifically accompanied this process with diverse aims: whether a popular open-air market or an aristocratic outdoors play-room, in any case they provided useful and required spaces for a colonized society maintaining even today its cultural and economic dependence on the metropolitan First-World, in an ongoing process of importing ways of life from abroad.

Buenos Aires' foundation followed Spanish settlement regulations for its American colonies, but during the nineteenth century great changes reflected French lights, plus Italian, German and English twinkles. The twentieth century appeared as an inexhaustible fountain of offers, again from Europe but also from the United States where new generations searched for identification.

Attempts to construct an identity of our own were minimized by the reigning mystique of the imported. This is not surprising as it started with our birth and feeds upon contradictory forces within our past known through The Official History.[10] The sequence of imposed viceroyalties, democratically elected governments and *de facto* dictatorships highly influenced the shape and use of our urban space, especially plazas.

The Spanish stereotype began from zero, from virgin territory, and that is why it is often confused with a root creator that we are supposed to respect as our own. Modernization through "French style" came to entirely modify that social and urban structure three centuries old, progressively effecting a real transculturalization ultimately accepted (in turn) as our own. Since the middle of the twentieth century, both local paradoxes and the contemporary complex world confused local park designers and builders who were not able to build adequate public promenades in quality and/or quantity (Fig. 17). A new change was given by the concrete post modernistic promenades built during the dictatorship period which were, and still are, the most clear urban icons of its ideology. The democracy rebirth in 1983 brought back the use of urban public space. But, nevertheless, the expected new undertakings for new times viewed as auspicious were more and more limited, scarce and poor. Corruption grew up to inconceivable levels, bad administrations continued.

Sometimes it is useful to lose the way, to enable the search for and choice of a new one. What will the river of life bring us in the future? Buenos Aires society as a whole has to find the answers.

Bibliography

Alphand, Adolphe and Baron Ernouf. *L'art des jardins*. Paris: Rothschild, c. 1875.

Alphand, Adolphe. *Les promenades de Paris*. Paris: Rotschild, 1867-1873.

Anonymous. *Caras y Caretas* 447 (April 27th, 1907) pages N. A.

Argentinean National Government. Congreso de la Nación. Diario de Sesiones. Buenos Aires: Congreso de la Nación, 1874. Sarmiento speech.

Berjman, Sonia, comp. *Benito Javier Carrasco: sus textos*. Buenos Aires: Facultad de Agronomía de la Universidad de Buenos Aires, 1997.

Berjman, Sonia, comp. *Carlos Thays: sus escritos sobre jardines y paisajes*. Buenos Aires: Ciudad Argentina, 2002.

Berjman, Sonia. "Forestier en la ciudad de Buenos Aires." In *Actes du Colloque international sur J. C. N. Forestier*. Edited by Bénédicte Leclerc. Paris: Picard, 1990, 207-219.

Berjman, Sonia. *La plaza española en Buenos Aires 1580-1880*. Buenos Aires: Kliczkowski, 2001.

Berjman, Sonia. *Plazas y parques de Buenos Aires, la obra de los paisajistas franceses*. Buenos Aires: Fondo de Cultura Económica, 1998.

Buenos Aires City Government. Comisión de Estética Edilicia. *Proyecto orgánico para la urbanización del municipio; el plano regulador y de reforma de la Capital Federal*. Buenos Aires: Peuser, 1925.

Buenos Aires City Government. *El nuevo plano de la ciudad de Buenos Aires. Informe del Arquitecto J.Bouvard*. Buenos Aires: Talleres Gráficos de la Penitenciaría Nacional, 1910.

Difrieri, Horacio. *Atlas de Buenos Aires*, Buenos Aires: Municipalidad de la Ciudad de Buenos Aires, no data.

Fevre, Fermín. *Serra-Valera: un nuevo paisaje urbano*. Buenos Aires: Ediciones Union Carbide, no data.

Gutiérrez, Ramón and Jorge Enrique Hardoy. "La ciudad hispanoamericana en el siglo XVI". Lecture in the Seminario La Ciudad Iberoamericana. Comisión de Obras Públicas y Urbanismo de España, Buenos Aires, November 1985, unpublished.

Gutiérrez, Ramón and Sonia Berjman. *La Plaza de Mayo, escenario de la vida argentina*. Buenos Aires: Fundación Banco de Boston, 1995.

Hobsbawn, Eric. *Años interesantes. Una vida en el siglo XX*. Buenos Aires: Planeta, 2003.

ICOMOS Heritage at Risk 2001 Report in www.icomos.org (Argentinean Section signed by Fabio Grementieri and Sonia Berjman).

Jarrasé, Dominique. "Le bouquet de Paris. Les jardins publics parisiens au XIX ème. siècle." *Monuments Historiques* 142 (1982).

Rípodas Ardanaz, Daisy. "Las ciudades indianas." In the *Atlas de Buenos Aires*, edited by Horacio Difrieri. Buenos Aires: Municipalidad de la Ciudad de Buenos Aires, no data.

Romero, José Luis. *Latinoamérica: las ciudades y las ideas*. Buenos Aires: Siglo Veintiuno, 1976.

Sarmiento, Domingo Faustino. *Civilisation et barbarie. Moeurs, coutumes, caractères des peuples argentins. Facundo Quiroga et Aldao*. Paris: Arthus Bertrand Éditeur, 1853.

Sarmiento, Domingo Faustino. *Civilización y barbarie. Vida de Juan Facundo Quiroga y aspecto físico, costumbres y hábitos de la República Argentina*. Santiago de Chile: Imprenta del Progreso, 1845.

Sarmiento, Domingo Faustino. *Life in the Argentine Republic in the Days of the Tyrants; or Civilization and Barbarism*. New York: Hurd and Houghton, 1868.

Vernes, Michel. "Génese et avatars du jardin public." *Monuments Historiques* 142 (1982).

Waisman, Marina. *La estructura histórica del entorno*. Buenos Aires: Nueva Vision, 1985.

Notes

[1] I am a Latin American woman from the very American South, great-grandchild of Jewish Ukrainian immigrants and a member of the Argentinean sixties' generation characterized by a strong French postwar influence.

[2] Santiago del Estero was the first city founded by Spaniards in the future Argentinean territory in 1553. We consider Buenos Aires one of the latest American cities founded through Spanish conquest. Buenos Aires was founded for the first time in 1536 but this enterprise failed, its founders literally eaten by the indigenous.

[3] Peruvian Viceroy Amat was the builder of Paseo de las Aguas and the Alameda de los Descalzos in Lima from 1770 to 1780.

[4] Thanks to a Dumbarton Oaks Grant given in 1995 to Sonia Berjman and Daniel Schávelzon we could gather a complete documentation archive about Palermo park.

[5] In the State of Massachusetts the Teacher's Day is celebrated – as in Argentina – the day of Sarmiento's death: September 11th.

[6] André established a wider and more ambitious park plan for Montevideo, Uruguay, in 1891.

[7] Eugéne Courtois. French, former gardener of l'Ecole de Médecine de Paris, he came to Argentina c. 1860.

[8] Bouvard also proposed City Plans for Rosario (Argentina), Montevideo (Uruguay) and Sao Paulo (Brazil).

[9] When I graduated from History of Art at the Universidad de Buenos Aires during the 1970's I could be thrown from a plane into Paris, and could easily have found my way, as learning was based in the European culture. Not even one subject of Latin American art was taught until the late 1980's.

[10] "The Official History" is *also* the title of an Argentinean film honored with an Oscar.

Gardens and Cultural
Change: A Pan-American
Perspective

Gardens and Cultural
Change: A Pan-American
Perspective

Gardens and Cultural
Change: A Pan-American
Perspective

Gardens and Cultural
Change: A Pan-American
Perspective

Parks and Democracy in a Growing City: Palermo, Buenos Aires

Daniel Schavelzon

There are many people who in spite of not
being completely submerged in barbarism,
are unaware of the need for gardens,
while others that are at the dawn of civilization,
would feel smothered should they not have
the chance to breathe the scent of flowers.

Juan de Cominges
Palermo until 1882

Those who visit the Palermo parks nowadays may feel surprised by the profusion of statues and grand monuments dedicated to militaries and civilians that once were closely related to the park. Such proliferation is not accidental and neither is the social compulsion for displaying in marble and bronze the memory of those who participated in the creation of a public space. The history of these monuments, the places they occupy, point to a record of political and military struggles for the control of the city that had this park as its core; it accumulates, like a mechanical condenser, the notions on how one society, one government and one city were supposed to work. Its physical structure reflects changes, progress and setbacks, together with intellectual and political issues that were solved, at times, through weapons and wars. Moreover, these changes also reflect how decisions were made regarding control of the population in a city that expanded and changed at a faster pace than the ruling capabilities of its leading classes. It is as well a long history of struggles in the pursuit of democracy and the ways it could be manipulated. The history of Palermo can be seen in the framework of the inclusion-exclusion processes of portions of the society in urban life both as a struggle for rights and for revealing how society determined the use of space.

We must imagine a city located in one of the southernmost zones in the world, a city that was emerging from almost three centuries of colonial domination and was receiving an immigration that would transform everything at a great speed. By the end of the nineteenth century more than three quarters of the population in Buenos Aires were first or second generation immigrants, or so were their parents. In 1813, the discussion around the partial freedom of enslaved Africans began, but in the city, full freedom was not achieved before 1861. Of the thirty five percent afrodescendents among the total population in 1800, only two percent were left in 1880, and American Indians were near one percent ten years later. Therefore, one generation later, the measures taken to prevent or encourage the use of urban spaces by these social groups would prove useless. In 1875, as the sole viable solution, attempts were being made to cut the country in two by means of a huge ditch that would separate the lands of the white (and afro) from those of the natives: the *Zanja de Alsina*; twenty years later and after a long war, those Indians were not even considered as existing human beings in the national census. How would it be possible to establish policies of use in a city undergoing changes so abrupt that escaped understanding, even at the time when they were taking place? Palermo is a part and an example of such history.

Sculptures and Spaces: The Materialization of Social Success

When visiting the older portion of Palermo, two major and two secondary monuments will be encountered, all visually and physically interconnected by wide avenues. The major one and probably the largest in dimensions in the city is the Monument to Independence (wrongly referred to, locally, as *Monumento a los Españoles*), presented by Spain in 1910 for the first centennial of Independence. An outstanding masterpiece of Art Nouveau by Agustín Querol, it creates a magnificent rond-point at the crossing of avenues; two of the corners in this crossroad feature the sculptures of Domingo F. Sarmiento (by Auguste Rodin) and Juan Manuel de Rosas (by Ricardo Dama Lasta), placed in very special spots above the remains of ancient, demolished architectural works that were used as foundations. They both created Palermo: one, Rosas, out of nothing; the other, Sarmiento, by returning all former works to nothingness and starting anew. At that time they fought one another and today, symbolically, they still stand as stone opponents pointing at each other with their extended arms. On the same avenue, his sword wielded towards Sarmiento's statue, there is a huge monument of granite and bronze recovered from old cannons to honor Justo Jose de Urquiza (a work by Renzo Baldi and Héctor Rocha), the man who defeated Rosas in 1852 and forced him to leave Palermo. Sarmiento had served in that army after years of writing against the mere existence of the park. This group of personalities sculpted in marble, granite and bronze, haunting the Monument to Independence and what it represented to each one of them is not accidental, and synthesizes the history of public spaces in the city.

Rosas and His Political Project in an "Almost" Non-European Park

Juan Manuel de Rosas, governor of Buenos Aires and simultaneously head of the National State, was at the very heart of these developments. A hero to some, a tyrant to others, from 1828 to 1852. He had first noticed the lands where he would build his residency when he settled there with a military detail. Shortly after, upon concentrating in his hands the entire political power, he made the decision to invest large amounts of money in building a suburban home surrounded by gardens where he would live with his family—and where in fact, he would rule: a place that would encompass private residential activities, headquarters for the government and landscaping, fit for activities such as gardening, farming, cattle raising, the development of industrial initiatives and for public entertainment. It was to be known as Palermo de San Benito and would become eventually one of the most amazing public parks in the continent. The name was chosen almost by accident, as the word "Palermo" had been given to the place by an old local dweller, but it was fit to complete it with "de San Benito," as a part of the strong political process of inclusion of the *Afro-porteños* in his policies and in social urban activities bringing them civil rights.

To that purpose he bought around 250 hectares of land located out of the city limits, subjected to frequent floodings caused by the nearby river and which were used at that time

Fig. 1. Caserón de Rosas and surrounding park, lithograph by León Pallière ca. 1845; the rivulet and willow trees reflect the rustic and natural design of the place.

to feed cattle and to sow. He left a house in the city after his wife's passing, and in 1838 settled there for good, in a new palace built and used until 1852 (Fig. 1). Interestingly, the residency known as El Caserón (the big house) was not the result of a particular architectural design but rather, of a series of transformations accomplished in the house of a German family, which was enlarged at least twice. The project was inorganic in nature and was directed by Rosas himself, assisted by a skilled builder and by an engineer for gardening and landscaping matters.

Why would he buy land so far away from town, of a poor quality, floodable and marginal, if he was in a position to afford a better option? This decision, which raised comments and gave way to extended controversies that persisted for one and a half centuries, is easily understood, considering the historic moment and Rosas' personality. He decided to buy land in the only location where wealthy families would never come near, in a marginal, forsaken, primitive and wild place, an expression of an aggressive and romantic attitude; a place closer to the image of the "American savage" than to the "civilized" and European-like features of his opponents. The Scotsman William MacCann, trader and traveler who came in 1842 wrote:

> Someone could ask why would he build such a house in a place like that. He did it with the purpose of overcoming two major obstacles: the construction works began during the French naval blockade, and as people were in a state of great agitation, he had attempted to raise their spirits with an exhibition of confidence in a solid future, and by erecting his house in a rather unfavorable location, he attempted to set to his fellow-citizens an example of that which could be accomplished whenever obstacles were to be overcome.[1]

Rosas wanted his palace and his lands to be an expression of his ideas and his quest for a commercial independence from Europe; therefore, the building was to leave aside all esthetic fashions to unfold instead a local formal image, based on the tradition of the Spanish architecture that had been adjusted throughout two centuries, to the region. Such was the message he

Fig. 2. Promenaders using the place as a public park; access would be restricted only by the later iron fence, lithograph by Kratzenstein 1855. The building shows its full massive scale.

delivered; the strength of the ideological message of independence and power was explicit. Today, we could ask ourselves whether it was at all possible, back then, to build a park and an architecture that were completely free of what was being designed in those days. This has generated different interpretations along the years. Similar to the architecture and the landscape design, the gardening relied heavily on plants and trees brought from all over the national territory, arranged following a pattern of an orthogonal grid, following the Hispanic-American tradition for roads and waterways. Conceptually, it attempted to be some kind of little South American Versailles with a few local, romantic traits: cattle was slaughtered on the spot, soldiers lit their fires and had their meals in the gardens, two powder and brick factories stood in place while leisure and military areas mingled and physical boundaries between his property and that of his neighbors were inexistent, in such a way that everyone was welcome to tour the place. The gardens were handsomely trimmed, and picturesque groves, together with clear open areas where the cattle grazed, could be visited.

The main building featured an architecture typical of the pampean region, although the Neoclassical influences, which could not be totally avoided, increased the ambivalent attitude in the site. Two seasons of archaeologic work in the field in 1985 and 1988[2] have also shown that even though the purpose was to stress the local traits—Rosas had declared war against France and England and several battles had been fought—the floors of the house were made of tiles brought from France, the porcelain of his tableware was French and his bottles were English and Dutch. The place had gardens, a zoo, a building for the military guard, a ship from the U.S. that had run aground and was transformed into a dancing hall, and groves designed for horse riding and promenading. Two long water streams were rectified and one of them was transformed into a water reservoir with recreation pools to swim, while a little steam boat navigated up and down the waterways, flanked by benches of Italian marble. The gardens were taken care of by people that Sarmiento, Rosas' political opponent, future president and founder of the subsequent park, would contemptuously refer to as "an army of Italian gardeners" for the ornamental trees and plants and the orchards of fruit trees and edible greens.[3]

All of it was privately-owned but had no physical delimitation, so anyone was allowed to get in and out of the fields; there are several descriptions of promenaders who met face to face with the governor while he was taking a walk with his family (Fig. 2). The public and the private had no boundaries and that pointed to a carefully studied attitude from Rosas towards all his buildings. To some, this was only demagogy to ingratiate himself with the people; to others it was a wise decision that evidenced his good will towards every sector of the new society born with the Independence, which offered no options for the recreation of the newly-born bourgeoisie. Samuel G. Arnold, a U.S. traveler who later became governor of Rhode Island, visited the site and praised the English "touch"; but Arnold hesitated in discomfort when Rosas took off his shirt to show him that his skin was completely white, a gesture he did not fully understand.[4]

The worse among Rosas numerous and powerful enemies, Sarmiento, would bitterly criticize this system of private spaces for public use, demanding the transformation of the works he contemptuously described as a "turkish seraglio" into something more useful to the community. His ideas were influenced by the public parks he had visited in France, England and the U.S., which were unknown here, and by his concept of the National State whereby the difference between the public and the private was strong, democratic but not patriarchal. But it should be noted that precisely this park-field-residency-industrial compound represented a very rare effort in Latin America to generate a different kind of spatial

Fig. 3. Water color painted by Juan Camaña in 1852; the artist attempted to show some areas of the park (National Historic Museum).

organization for an open space. This project was conducted adjacent to a city where only the plazas inherited from the Spanish domination existed, with only one urban promenade by the river. Those plazas were used only as marketplaces, for official ceremonies, or as wagon parkings, with the subsequent display of noise, dirt, people sleeping in the open or eating their meals wherever they pleased; the original *raison d'être* of these plazas was not leisure. The Afros and *criollos* would use these spaces for socializing, dancing, and getting together in communities, thus banning the participation of whites. Only the old Plaza Mayor, eventually turned into stronghold and market, stood the chance to be used otherwise, though never for the rituals of recreation but for public ceremonies.[5]

The park was designed following Rosas' pragmatic instructions, with the assistance of the engineer Nicolás Descalzi and the constructor Miguel Cabrera. Everyone would be welcome as a part of the project, particularly the *Afro-porteños*—Africans born in Buenos Aires—to whom the San Benito chapel had been consacrated, in the palace backside. The name of the park stressed the close relationship existing with that particular group, as they had proved permanent supporters of Rosas' policies. But in a broader sense, the area was frequently visited by upper-class-white *criollos* during the weekends. When the land was selected and purchased, an environmental concept was worked out in an area comprising 535 hectares, although with the exception of a few topographical modifications, the nature of the place was not altered and the existing waterways were included. The riverside that the Spaniards in the past had totally disregarded was integrated and a special area preserved for growing fruit trees, while the forestation was respected and the first city zoo in the country was created. In addition, a military quarter was built, together with a powder factory, a slaughterhouse and kilns (Fig. 3). Even though there are no plans or records of this project, everything points to engineer Nicolás Descalzi who, always following Rosas' instructions and together with Miguel Cabrera, would constantly supervise the works.[6]

The landscape design displayed simplicity and austerity, contrasting with the gardens of the Neoclassical or historicistic *estancias* of those days; there were no tangible precedents and no specific European trend was pursued, though the design was not alien to the world of those times. In regard to the moderate originality of these works, MacCann stated:

> I assumed it would be surrounded by woods, prairies and other quarters typical of country houses, but instead, it looked like a plain space with several new plantations by the riverside (...) the land is so low that the landscape will hardly allow any picturesque character.[7]

No doubt, it was not the romantic or picturesque landscape regarding artifice that was traditional in Europe and which a Scotsman might expect. Yet, the spirit of the surroundings in this *Caserón* was undoubtedly related to the bucolic life of the pampean fields, a man-nature bond that included practical agricultural aspects, thus generating a style with characteristics of its own. Aesthetics were of a lesser significance, just a subsidiary concern.[8]

The recuperation of the floodable lands was slow, difficult and unprecedented. The works began in 1837 and were concluded in 1840, a project of a dimension never seen before in the country. Neverthelesss, the works were later bitterly criticized:

> Let's leave aside the Egyptian work of refilling with earth carried from far away a low and muddy field, and the thousands of arms poorly paid throughout eight years of work. The accountings of the treasury show that four million pesos were requested from the public treasury for Palermo, not to mention the registered seven million given to Pedro, to Juan, and to others commissioned to obtain funds from the cashboxes to fulfill the corresponding orders, not to mention the millions (...) from the State used in Palermo for the gardens destined to the recreation of the tyrant.[9]

As usual, what was being discussed was not the quality or the character of the works accomplished in the place, not even the aesthetics; the issue had to do with the use Rosas gave to the place. It was evident that the physical space was the materialization of a strong personal policy and not merely of aesthetic ideals.

Palermo's orthogonal scheme was basic for the roads, waterways, plantations and even the house, though the scheme would be slightly altered in recreational areas such as the gardens, where fountains, flowers, gazebos, birds and animals would mingle, or in the network of roads and paths designed to circulate in recreational areas. The design originated in the existing pragmatic lane scheme and in the Núñez-Hornung-Holterhoff house, after which the Caserón was built. The house was the core of the new residency, and it stood at the crossing of two roads which eventually would become large avenues, still existing to this date. With that crossroad as starting point, the lots were arranged in the form of four large sectors. It would take too long to describe the entire place: there were rectified and even artificial streams, an area of waterways and bridges where fruit trees were grown, a garden of magnolias and other flowers, a boat restored into a dancing hall, a long avenue flanked by willow trees that led to the riverside, an embarkment area and promenading zone, and the islet for resting (the governor's favorite), while among the trees, the zoo cages had been placed. At west the servants' quarters were located, together with a building known as *La Maestranza,* used by the army and with workshops for different manufactures, stables, a hospital and a pharmacy. There were also two Classic buildings where the roads crossed, one of them being a theater. Across the street in front of the Caserón the kitchen had been placed, facing the gardens there was a chinaberries grove.

The issue of how to handle water was an additional problem to solve, because besides the watering systems, the navigable ways and the drinkable water supply, a water surface was made, together with a pond for Manuelita, Rosas' daughter. This was organized by means of two hydraulic interconnected systems. The first was formed by the Manso stream, the reservoir, Manuelita's pond and two long ditches; the second, by the Maldonado stream and the watering canals for the fruit trees located in the northern sector. The streams were used for

Fig. 4. Model built based on pictures and archaeological remains, recreating the architecture of the central building by the time it was being used by Juan Manuel de Rosas until 1852. (Center for Urban Archaeology, University of Buenos Aires).

drainage, landscape and recreation; the main canal, for instance, was navigated by several boats and a steamship. To this day, the system has not substantially changed, except that now it stretches in pipes underground; even the idea of lakes to compensate the floods remains the same. The works to prepare the marshlands were truly original, and proof of that are the 6000 meters of the waterway's network. The reservoir compound was formed by the water surface, the terrace, a deck, a bathing resort, Manuelita's pond and the promenading meadows. All of these works were planned for leisure, an inexistent notion in the private residencies of those days. The pier was long enough to moor several boats and penetrated into the reservoir; there were stairs leading to the bathing resort, fenced with wooden rods to provide some privacy to the bathers, particularly the females. Vicuña Makena contemptuously noted: "Rosas and his daughter would bathe together in plain daylight and in front of the guards, because Manuelita Rosas, the Empress of El Plata, could allow herself to say, like the other Roman one when she bathed in the presence of her slave, 'This is not a man!'[10]. Eduardo Schiaffino, the art expert, had half century later a poor concept of the promenade and stated that the circuit was probably too short for a steamship and that it was equivalent to "navigating on a pony." The terrace was probably a place to rest and opened to the river; it was broad and shaded by willow trees that separated it from the road and the Caserón and they must have had a splendid view.[11]

When Rosas bought the first portion of land in Palermo, only a humble little house existed there, and a small waterway. Later, he bought a farmhouse from Carlota Núñez de Holterhoff. It had six rooms and it must have been a quality construction, considering that Rosas instructed Miguel Cabrera to proceed with the new building preserving the arrangement of the rooms. The final building, a ground plan with a flat roof, was symmetrical, square, with a central patio embraced by wide galleries with full centered arches. The observer could easily identify the building as a construction similar to most of the regional, traditional architecture common in the seventeenth and eighteenth centuries, a blend of Spanish traditions and locally

acquired features. A more careful observation shows some Neoclassical elements, particularly in the plan, which due to its simplicity, modulation and the presence of four projecting corners, resembles some palaces of the Italian Renaissance.[12]

The genealogy of the building has been the cause of heated controversies among the historians of local architecture, and the lack of documents has represented an additional problem (Fig. 4). In the old days it was a controversial issue too, and Sarmiento would ask himself:

Is there an architecture by Rosas? During his long ruling the domestic architecture took some specific shapes, it crystallized and then stopped. The entire block of the Government House and Palermo repeat an identical scheme, the terrace roof, crowned with iron fences instead of balusters. The whole city imperceptibly conveys the order of the day. Red doors, flat roofs and fences, pillars each three varas on the sidewalks. There are no two-story buildings, shapes don't change, there are no architects but simple masons.[13]

Fig. 5. Manuelita Rosas and her *Budoir Federal*, painted by Nicolás Descalzi possibly in 1848; the fireplace echoes the European tradition, together with the porcelain cups and vases, while the guitar, the "*mate*" and her father's portrait reflect the local tradition.

To the European-oriented critique, the sight of brick floors, plastered and white painted walls, rubblework benches, plain moldings and flat roofs with no garrets was simply disgusting.

The more reasonable historiographic opinion in this debate refers to the existence of a *national architecture* that saw the light during Rosas' time, one that was clearly opposed to what had been previously built during Rivadavia's administration by his French, English and Spanish technicians. The new style conveyed an ideological message rather than a mere aesthetic preference.[14] This national architecture would be a synthesis between an almost atemporal classicism and the *criollo,* pragmatic tradition born from the popular know-how and the domestic practices of building organizations—a synthesis which probably extended to the landscape configuration. To what degree the European Neoclassicism was immersed in this project is hard to say: no doubt, the construction was the result of sheer empiricism—there was no conscientious project, no professional architect—although the spirit of those days is present. There was an historiographic trend that suggested it was an adaptation of the Villa Poggio Reale in Naples, built by Giuliano da Sangallo,[15] reinterpreted by the local builder, and not the consequence of a localistic political will. Ramón Gutiérrez has stated: "No doubt, the expressive simplicity and a gravitating volumetry in the landscape bring us back to a morphologic proposal alien to the caprices of the pseudo-Napoleonic mannerisms of the Rivadavian period."[16] To others, however, the fact that the building maintained the colonial tradition in shape and distribution, with some economic aspects included, is not far from some French scholars of those times, Durand for instance, who might well have inspired the reticular structure of the plan. It is not by accident that Rosas avoided to draw any attention on his offices or his bedroom, or that there were no dressing rooms next to his daughter's quarters (as neither were there rooms for the servants, which were separated from the compound), or that his own office had worked both as dining room and living room (Fig. 5). To some, this responded to the austere Rosist spirit; to others, it was nothing but pretended plainness and close relationship with the people:

Fig. 6. Plan sketched by Gustavo Sordeaux, 1850, showing the Caserón, together with other nearby buildings and the even scheme of the park, the water canals and the groves.

> The issue of a necessary transparency in the space organization of this political project, assuming the restorer's confessed assumption that his is a public life contrasting with the results of anarchy, seems to find, in the Caserón, its perfect space of accomplishment (...); the private appears willingly transformed into public space. It is not by accident that Palermo displays such an original blend of park, rustic villa (that is, productive) and place of economical exploitation that materially express the character of the Rosist system, the confluence of economical and political power seen as the only way to leave behind anarchy and to ensure the expansion and growth of the new economic system of cattle exploitation (...). Rosas' and Manuelita's quarters are not carefully isolated from the public space. That is why, when analizing the Caserón's plan, Sarmiento is surprised to observe that the governor's daughter lacks servants' quarters next to her room, and some chroniclers mention that the residency in Palermo was so easily reached that in the last period of the decade of 1840, the Caserón had almost become a public space. Rosas could be observed in his daily life, and such was precisely his program.[17]

The second historiographic debate in force has to do with the authorship of the building, of which no plans or documents are available. Actually, many important local and foreign architects with the skills necessary to design such a project were active in the city. Historiography mentions Felipe Senillosa in the first place, Rosas' favorite, whom several historians have pointed as the author.[18] Another well-known personality of those days was José Santos Sartorio, an Italian builder who as a consequence of the support Rosas gave him, was given the nickname of "architect of the tyranny." In 1836 he was appointed Government Architect and Master Builder of the City;[19] he probably meddled somehow, though in no way he was in a position to be fully in charge, because he suffered a severe mental illness and was committed before the works had come to an end. Finally, Miguel Cabrera represents the most recent historiographic advance; some documents and information have been found which confirm his participation in the Caserón. The details of his career are not abundant, but at least it is known that between 1841 and 1847 he was at Rosas' personal service in Palermo, as the builder and administrator of the entire compound.[20]

Rosas had there a full rural establishment, although, interestingly, the accounts of visitors fail to mention this detail; we do not know whether this was out of sight, or they'd rather not become aware of this kind of activity parallel to the others of ruling and entertaining.[21] But we know now that cattle was slaughtered, hides were treated, there were plantations of fruit trees, and in December, 1845, there was a total of 259 individuals, working not as servants in the Caserón and not for the government organization.

Then we ask ourselves who really used the park, how, and what for. These are complex questions with no definite answers. We know, thanks to the writers of those times, that all social activities concentrated in Palermo, that diplomats were frequently seen there, like Count Colonna Walewsky, Napoleon's son, Prince Bentivoglio, the brother of Countess Walewsky, Count Mareuil and the military staff of missions appointed by the courts of France and England. During the gatherings, politics were left aside, and the evenings unfolded with poetry recitals, quiz games, picnics in the groves or concerts in the hall-boat (Fig. 6). Visitors and chroniclers speak of horseback ridings, boat tours, gatherings under the trees and fishing. We also know that wealthy families went there for long weekend stays, as the place was quite far from town and at least a carriage or a horse were required. And we assume that meeting face to face with the governor and other personalities must have been a part of the social interplay. We know as well that Rosas encouraged the attendance of the Afro population through the name given to the place and the chapel dedicated to San Benito, though we lack any further information concerning other lower class groups. However, the presence in illustrations of soldiers, drivers and other characters, shows that visitors were heterogeneous, and when observing the way soldiers took their meals at the park, we come to the conclusion that good manners were not a characteristic of the times; and that if these were, Rosas should be feeling greatly pleased for breaking them. He was at all times the "savage barbarian" identified with his people; that image was not designed by his opponents, it was encouraged by himself.

After Rosas: Negotiation, Resistence, and Design

Rosas' government, unquestionably dictatorial and despotic, had to face a strong opposition. It was a heterogeneous opposition and one that pursued different interests, though basically discussions were focused around ceasing to be a federation of states ruled by regional *caudillos* to start building a modern nation. This implied the loss of the sovereignty of the states to erect Buenos Aires like a capital city where wealth and power would be concentrated. Most of the best European-oriented intellectuals of those days were against the governor, particularly Domingo F. Sarmiento, who with writing after writing disqualified Rosas and all his doings, including Palermo, his home, the refills of the lowlands and the mixed activities of leisure and production that took place in his grounds. The power necessary for a systematic military struggle was achieved by Justo J. de Urquiza, who would in turn build for himself a huge rural house surrounded by elegant parks, although the entire architecture was clearly French-like. Urquiza succeeded in organizing an army with the support of Brazil and European mercenaries to finally overthrow Rosas in 1852, after several armed confrontations. A few years later, he would also be assassinated.

Rosas' military defeat led the way to the first government interested in the creation of a modern and democratic National State, very different from the old Rosist patriarchal notions. This generated endless controversies around the future use of his lands, while the building was destined to public uses. Rosas' power collapsed so abruptly that for quite some time no one came up with a proposal regarding his former home. The first firm measure was the confiscation of his entire estate; voices raised in anger because it was unclear whether the Nation or the city would retain the rights on those properties. Besides, it had to be determined if his heirs were or were not entitled to keep the estate. The latter decision was made by president Urquiza, who passed the entire estate to Rosas' attorney, his son-in-law Terrero, who moved to the Caserón and simultaneously sold out several *estancias*. Accounts report that 700 wagons with different objects from the Caserón were taken away. Shortly after, the province of Buenos Aires was separated from the rest of the Confederation, and the new legislative power declared that no previous act from the National Congress would be acknowledged; consequently, Terrero was forced to give the Caserón back, which was then abandoned for a while.

It was only in 1858 when the Caserón recovered its former fame when it housed the first exhibition of cattle breeders and industries, an example of the new public and social use the place would have. Sarmiento, inspired in the Great London Exhibit of 1855 and its Crystal Palace, said:

> Palermo is admirably adaptable to the most grandiose plan of industrial exhibition. Its square of buildings enclosed within a wide patio with huge aljibes is fit to receive one day a crystal roof, to protect, with no restrictions of light or heat, the countless plants, flowers and bushes that already enrich our collections of flowers, while the four warehouses that the creativeness of the rancher and architect placed at the edges of his singular dwelling, to provide the petitioners, soldiers and courtiers with some shade, may be adapted to collections of birds, animals or other objects (...). Palermo will, thus, be transformed into a subject of public interest, emerging from that sort of curse that fell upon it and which doomed it to inevitable destruction; and the monuments of the savage tyranny turned, like the Model School and the Industrial Exhibition, into instruments of civilization and progress, as an appropriate revenge of the people he sought to enslave.[22]

Actually, the show was modest, inasmuch as the First Agricultural, Rural and Industrial Exhibition ever carried out in South America occupied two halls only: one with products of agriculture, and the other with manufactures; animals were placed at the patio and just one iron machine was exposed at all. The difference with the great London show was there for all to see. The ideological and political struggle still prevailed and science, culture or production were secondary issues. According to *Los Debates*: "The exhibition was inaugurated yesterday (...) inspired by the contrast between the joyfull display of this pacifying and civilizing effort of industry, and the one of tyranny presented not too long ago in the same hall."[23]

Discussions around the property continued, and in 1856 the estate was passed over to the town of Belgrano, created, precisely, in Rosas' former lands. President Sarmiento attempted to put an end to this issue with a decree by which the funds obtained from the sale were to be applied to new school buildings. Consequently, the School of Arts and Crafts and Agronomy were born. In 1865 a military section was established there and it remained there until 1868. The following year, the Military

College was created, and it occupied completely the building and its lands; thus, the Caserón, which had been built to house one single family and its servants, became the home of 118 cadets, plus all officers, professors, troopers and service personnel (Fig. 7).[24] It continued there until 1892, when it would house the new Military Naval School, which was kept as such until the building was blown up in 1899.

This stage of unfulfilled projects is consistent with the age: the city and the country changed abruptly, the Afro population was fading at a quick pace, and the Indians were

Fig. 7. Military drills after Rosas overthrow, disregarding that wide avenues had been opened and that major buildings still stood in place. Picture taken around 1879 (General Archives of the Nation).

being brutally exterminated in the struggles for taking their territories away from them, the new immigration posed new challenges and public spaces were an image of the new State and social modelers with new characteristics: the end of that Palermo that once belonged to Rosas was the end of a pattern of collective organization. The new society that was being born, confusing and heterogeneous, made it difficult to make decisions. But it was a society in which two of the major interlocutors were starting to be missing: Indians and Afros, and a society that looked insistently to Europe and the massive immigration arriving therefrom.

The Creation of the New Palermo Park: A New Space for a New Society

Absurd as it may seem, Palermo is a nonexistent word in the established urban terminology. The park we have been referring to from the very beginning bears the illogical name of *Parque 3 de Febrero,* one with which not even the local population is familiar. The memory is so strong that after 150 years of trying, the name could not be changed.

Following Rosas' fall, Sarmiento led the huge task of creating in those lands a new, totally different public park, though the location would not be changed. He had to face a stubborn opposition from those who resisted recuperating the lands that once belonged to Rosas, and those who believed that the State was not to invest funds in this kind of enterprise. An inspection of the controversy, cruel and complex, shows that the major protagonists lacked any solid knowledge of the situation. And for years the project was delayed with silly arguments which ultimately only evidenced a poor imagination and a late hatred for a place that had been nothing more than a scenario for political events. Sarmiento, at that time as president and later as director of the works, never failed to encourage the project of the park. In 1874, finally, the park was officially inaugurated.

The first project was won by Carlos Boermel and Adolf Methfessel but did not prosper: Carlos Dormal with a second project initiated the works, but because of the elevated costs of Dormal's project, this was handed over to Jordan Czeslaw Wysoscki. It was not by accident that all of them were Europeans, like the French Fernand Mauduit and the Prussian Ernst Oldendorff. In 1875 the first portion of the new park was inaugurated, although in the following years the works would be interrupted, reinitiated and quite too often delayed. By 1881, the wide accessing avenue, presently Avenida del Libertador, was finally made anew, and in 1892 the Botanical Garden was inaugurated when Carlos Thays was appointed Director of Parks and Promenades and devoted himself completely to this project[25] (Fig. 8). From then on, the works continued uninterruptedly until 1939, when the park met its full extension.

Why so much insistence on a new design for the park, destroying what was already there? There were different interpretations on what was to be done, but everyone agreed on one thing: the landscape, as opposed to the building, was not to be preserved as it was. True, international trends had changed and French landscaping was remarkably popular in Argentina and the world, but there was much more to it: it was the meditated fracture of the urban design, of the square grid with which the entire city had been built, with the allegation that in that way the lands of "barbarism" would become "civilized." Thus, the notion was born that the original territory conveyed a meaning of barbarism as opposed to its counterpart, European gardens. It did not matter that Palermo was also the product of one design, it was savage for the mere fact of not being designed after the French or English traditions. Thus, the new Palermo was increasingly becoming a symbol of antibarbarism, a vehicle to civilize, it was the transformation of landscape

Fig. 8. Plan sketched in 1897 showing changes in Palermo occurred by the late XIX century. The plots of land grew larger and were designed anew; the Caseron still stood, at the crossroad.
Fig. 9. The romantic ideal of the new Palermo: a Venice in Latin America, postcard by Salvatore Liguri, 1885.

and society altogether[26] (Fig. 9). If the society of Spanish colonial times had designed a square gridded city, it had to be changed because the city changes society, and because if society had changed, the city had to change as well. Perhaps what was not clear to Sarmiento and other intellectuals was the difference between the French garden with its "regulated behaviors" and the English one, romantic and irregular; each type of park is the representation of ideal models of behavior for different societies.

After 1874 Rosas' memory had begun to fade in his gardens although not in his residency; the parks had a gateway to regulate the access and wide avenues to tour it, and the first norms of use were established (Fig. 10). Agricultural activities, cattle breeding, and other productive aspects had vanished, while the gardening for leisure and recreation was in its dawn, but memory, somehow, remained. The State had clearly defined its limits and functions and the park was to express them, moreover, it had to help build it. Juan de Cominges described the social need of the new park:

> Where were the wealthy bachelors of the upper classes in the city supposed to display their handsome gallantry and the gracefulness of their spirited steeds? Where were the opulent matrons to show their trunks, their carriages, their liveries, their jewelry, their elegance and their noble kindness? Where, in the leisure days, would the humble day-laborer go to cheer his spirit promenading among flowers and enjoying with his family a modest asado under the shadow of plants? (…) As to the proletarian classes, whose habits are slowly becoming sweeter, thanks to some civilizing institutions, among which the park is found at the head of the line (…) If the proletarian classes do not visit the Palermo park with the desired frequency, let's not put the blame on the distance that separates it from Buenos Aires; let's put the blame in the first place on the state of their culture, which does not allow them to enjoy the very pure pleasures that the sight of beauty provides.[27]

Fig. 10. Opening of the new road to Palermo with its large gates; note the wild environment. It was a part of Sarmiento's great project to build everything anew for public use but with a restricted access (General Archives of the Nation).

A New Controversy: To Demolish or Not to Demolish?

Rosas' home, the building not the park, remained in a somewhat good condition in spite of the repeated changes in its use and the transformations in its surroundings. But in 1899 a new debate began, which would once more divide the Buenos Aires society: was it to be demolished or not? The controversy was out of control because what was being discussed was a matter of pure politics over two different issues: the limits of the municipal power over the symbols of the past admitted or despised according to each one's point of view, and what it meant to make *tabula rasa* on the unwanted past. The building was to be destroyed to widen the grand avenue that connected the park with the city, a monumental axis for the carriages of the urban aristocracy.

Those who supported the destruction of all the vices of the past would say:

> Many have referred to the convenience of demolishing the old Palermo: some others believe that the relic should be preserved for the education of the generations to come, so that they may learn, by contemplating it, to repudiate

dictatorships (...): we have never shared that point of view because (...) whenever the relics of the past do not represent, like the ruins of Greece or Rome or even of Mexico and Cuzco, a great artistic or archaeological interest, there is no reason to insist in keeping a vulgar construction, devoid of all architectural character, of which hundreds of examples exist in the country, and finally, the sight of which only brings back memories of blood, crime, oppression and barbarism.[28]

Another newspaper read: "Not one brick will remain of the old Rosas' house (...) and its flat, vulgar body will no longer spoil the perspective of the park and the avenues, nor will it bring back the memory of a barbarian past (...). It was not good enough to have used the place for the higher purposes of intellectual interest for the Army to clear away the sinister remembrance it evoqued."[29]

Those who defended the building and its surroundings felt it was an act of barbarism to tear it down, and were as well driven by nostalgia, by early preservationist notions or merely by their opposition to the government:

We have a criollo municipal mayor, who, with a vindicative spirit, celebrates the anniversary of a political event of some importance in the history of our social evolution by using his workers and his picks to demolish an old building, full of suggestion and typical, characteristic of an age, powerfull searchlight to the wise men who study and rescue from the monuments, silent to the majority, surprising truths; in Europe, those official picks remove the earth to discover a city covered with lava (...). It has escaped from previous actions, and was repeatedly saved by the deeds of Mitre, Sarmiento, Avellaneda, whose cultured spirits were sensitive to those flat walls, those colonial-looking arcades, those little pillars resembling chimneys, that pretentious compound which nontheless represented a monument in the eyes of the gauchos, used to the narrow and long chorizo ranch or the quincho walls (...), that house symbolized their orgy of freedom and parody of government (...), it was the wild pampa, knife in hand, claiming for its rights, it was the history of one's country, the origin of the Argentine people (....) they are going to kick down something that the wise men of the future will find very hard to rebuild.[30]

In any case, for the celebration of a new anniversary of Rosas' fall, during the night of February 2 to 3, 1899, the building was blown up with dynamite in the middle of a party that came to an end with the sunlight. Incidentally, during the archaeological excavations of 1985, remains of that celebration were recovered.[31] Thus, every apparent bit of the past and of Rosas' government was closed, but they forgot that memory is stronger than physical events, and the word Palermo was never to be replaced.

A single irrelevant detail: Manuelita's and Rosas' favorite tree was torn apart, in spite of the fact that it was a famous tree at that time because under its shade, legend has it, the sentences passed against the dictator's enemies were commuted. The mayor of the city gave to the U.S. Ambassador, W.J. Buchanan, a cane made of the wood of that tree; the ambassador in turn wrote him a note requesting that the cane bear the allegorical inscription "Souvenir of Don Juan Manuel de Rosas' dictatorship" on a silver ribbon.

Fig. 11. First section of the park inaugurated by Sarmiento around 1890, with new rivulets, pergolas and iron bridges (General Archives of the Nation).
Fig. 12. The new function: one of the lakes, with swans and boats, in a bucolic late afternoon (General Archives of the Nation, 1915).

Who Were Allowed to Use the Park and Who Were Not

In addition to such decisions and gardening developments, another heated controversy was initiated around the access to the park, raising conflict between different social groups and protests from anarchists and socialists.[32] Up until then, the issue had been used by Rosas to provide the Afro population with a physical space, taking them out of the city and inserting them in his own residency, even though simultaneously he would invite the very best of the local society, who promenaded in a boat along his canals and streams. Sarmiento, who would become the creator of the new park and the promoter of this kind of space in the city, believed in a park open to all without differentiations. He was caught in an idealization and utopia that never existed, as those were the years of extermination and extinction of the non-white human groups; everyone was welcome, but actually only those who were the winners visited the place. A wonderful and beautiful park was inaugurated, (Fig. 11) almost totally different from the former one, but what had also changed was society and its composition; by the time it was inaugurated the country was receiving thousands and thousands of white immigrants, Indians were being fought, and Afros erased away.

Sarmiento, a strong promoter of European immigration, in his final years observed with concern that things were not quite that simple: to terminate the Indians and to bring in Europeans would not solve the problems of the country. Not all Europeans were the same: the newcomers were illiterate Spanish, Arabian or Italian laborers, and not intellectuals, scientists and industrial entrepreneurs. And these differences began to become apparent as those groups started to demand access to public spaces and the upper classes demanded in turn their own differentiated places (Fig.

12). Palermo once again was the center of controversies and the restricted accesss involved more complicated issues than the mere design of a space: since the State could no longer forbid the entrance to all too explicitly, other more sophisticated systems began to operate. This was finally settled with the creation of two additional parks in the poorer southern and western areas of the city, designed to be used by the lower and middle classes so that Palermo could be preserved for the delight and enjoyment of the upper bourgoisie. Like a chronicler put it: "The Sarmiento avenue is, in fact, an aristocratic hall with proportions enough to contain the upper bourgoisie of Buenos Aires"[33] (Fig. 13). With the new accessing avenue Palermo inaugurated gateways, and even though there were no real enclosing fences, it was no longer open like it was in Rosas' days, or like other plazas in the city. A park had been built for the enjoyment of all, but time came to show that in the past, as a private park everyone was welcome but now that it was public, access was restricted in several subtler ways. It was closed with social barriers; it was permeable, but to many, it felt alien. According to a description of Rosas days, "it was easy to get close to him: one only had to get near his residency and go to Palermo, where access was not difficult, as it had become a public promenade."[34]

This controversy, encouraged by

Fig. 13. Wide concourse denominated "Avenida Sarmiento" as of 1889, used by the grand local bourgeoisie; it was one of the first places with artificial lights in the city (engraved in Paris, collection of the author).
Fig. 14. One park avenue on a Sunday, when the local bourgeoisie promenaded by car in the 1920s; note the watchman leaning on the sculpture at front, reading (General Archives of the Nation).

defenders of a new way of participatory democracy that included the free vote, was a part of the new democratization of the use of the public by all ethnic and social groups, once the Indians and the black people had been exterminated. In the speech Sarmiento pronounced when the park was inaugurated, he stated: "Only in a vast, artistic and accessible park the people will be people."[35] But the society was already European, non- racially heterogeneous like in Rosas' days; now the differences were only social.

For many years the poor had a restricted access and were sometimes invited away after they had managed to get in; the use of a cap instead of a hat, or having unpolished shoes, were reasons enough to be taken away by the many guards that watched over the place. In most parks in the country regulations were established and quite strict norms were in force, though this did not prevent some fugitive killer from taking refuge in the park, or becoming a night shelter for the homeless. In addition to being the core of such discussions, it was also the scenario of a number of specific actions that required evaluation by a society undergoing an urbanization process towards modernity. Palermo was considered modernity in itself, and at the same time a laboratory where changes were observed and theories adjusted for the new social order. Sarmiento was aware of the *civilizing* effect parks had, as homogenizers of social differences, as providers of some sun and light, of free access, of social hygiene. But for the poor it was too far away. True, that changed with time, but back then the reaction was strong and incomprehension remarkable.

From the very beginning, the urban aristocracy took possession of the park for promenading in carriages in what was known as *El Corso*. This was a round, pre-established tour in luxurious horse-carriages, where the important families would greet one another, criticize one another or show-off their outfits before the eyes of others. There were specific hours, garments, colors and even special ways of greeting one another, as well as mechanisms to prevent the participation of undesirable visitors. On the 8th of October, 1882, one thousand and three hundred carriages paraded.

In 1901, in a charity event, a group of two hundred young people who had bought their tickets were withdrawn from the place by the police, simply because "their shoes were not patent leather and they wore no gloves or top hat."[36] The social chronicle of the day reported that "they were poor fellows who believed they had the right to breath a little oxygen."[37] This was the naked truth underlying a magnificent project of *social hygiene* that ended up the defensive stronghold of a particular group: the park would only be for them for many years to come; the others could keep the humble urban plazas.

Sarmiento, not by accident Rosas' major enemy, was the one that transformed the place and saved it; with a different design and with a different purpose, but he preserved it. True, his ideas were not too distant from Humboldt's thinking about preserving the legacy of *"savagery"* as a lesson to the future, but what he wanted, or what he needed as the ideologist of a new kind of society, was a place to accomplish the changes he wanted for that society, a testing space to promote the new way of life (Fig. 14). Palermo served as such so that the components of an increasingly conflictive city, one that was about to explode could be neutralized through infusion of the new ideals, to achieve the consolidation of a new National State. The park was the *artifact* (a term with a clear etymology), the apparent catalyst which, in front of the city and its vices, would change it and make it more habitable.

Recent History: Returning To The Past

As aristocracy established sanctuaries of their own far from this park, throughout the twentieth century, Palermo—now open to the entire community and with its grand gateways torn down, social struggles long gone—was to endure a new serious and increasingly heated controversy. Early in the twentieth century, the State began to give away land, in dubious maneuver, to sport clubs and other varied institutions, in a way that throughout the years came to transfer almost its original surface. The situation, shaded by sixty years of dictatorships during which decisions were not even reported, came to light with the return of democracy, drawing public attention early in the decade of 1990, when an accelerated dismembering of the park began to take place. Government corruption and inefficiency caused that large portions of its surface were turned over to private hands, and used as parking lots for garbage trucks, or for driving practices, for bars, and for the opening of countless paved streets and highways. The struggle to recuperate a significant portion of these lands rested, once again, on the community, now organized by non-governmental institutions, which restored to the park the democratic significance it once used to have.

This situation caught the attention of Dumbarton Oaks, and funds were granted by the *Center for Landscape Architecture* in 1995[38] for the study of this situation and the creation of a documentary archive on the whole process, before the evident loss of one of the grand parks of the world. The problem, to this day, remains unsolved, and it is still the core of a controversy between the municipal state and society, which failed to overcome the strong politization that the place underwent in the mid-nineteenth century. There are two striking issues: first, "Palermo" is still the name recognized by all, although officially there is a different name printed on the plans, for the confusion of tourists;[39] second, during the excavation works (in 1985 and 1988) the archaeological team was brutally attacked and beaten, first by Rosas' and later by Sarmiento's followers.

Notes

[1] William MacCann, *Viaje a Caballo por las provincias argentinas* (Buenos Aires: Emecé, 1939).

[2] Daniel Schavelzon, *The Historical Archaeology of Buenos Aires* (New York: Kluwer-Academic-Plenum Press, 2000).

[3] Jorge Ramos and Daniel Schavelzon, Historia y Arqueología de Palermo de San Benito. Aspectos de su planeamiento ambiental, *Anales del Instituto de Arte Americano* 27-28 (1989-1991): 74-92; Marco Rufino, La Casa de Rosas, Palermo de Garay a la Actualidad, *Todo es Historia* 253 (1986):72-97; Horacio Pando, Palermo de San Benito, *Anales del Instituto de Arte Americano* 17 (1964): 51-63.

[4] Samuel G. Arnold, *Viajes por America del Sur* (Buenos Aires: Emece Editores, 1951).

[5] Sonia Berjman, *La plaza española en Buenos Aires 1580-1880* (Buenos Aires: Kliczkowski Editor, 2001).

[6] This documentary finding is recent; it can be seen in Jorge Ramos, *Miguel Cabrera, la hacienda de San Benito de Palermo y el Caserón de Palermo de San Benito* (Buenos Aires: Unpublished text, 1986) and in Ramos and Schavelzon, *Historia y Arqueología* (1989-1991); Carlos Fresco, Los hacedores de la quinta de Rosas en Palermo de San Benito, *La Gaceta de Palermo* 6 (1987): 8-13; Carlos Fresco, La casona de Rosas y el maestro Miguel Cabrera, *La Gaceta de Palermo* 5 (1986): 11-14. The way Rosas conducted the works can be seen in Lucio V. Mansilla, *Rozas: ensayo histórico psicológico* (Buenos Aires: Editorial Belgrano, 1967); Adolfo Saldías, *Historia de la Confederación Argentina* (Buenos Aires: EUDEBA, 1968) II: 372-373.

[7] William MacCann, *Viaje a Caballo* (1939): 48.

[8] For descriptions of Palermo: Marco Rufino, La casa de Rosas (1986); Roberto Boracchia, *Palermo o San Benito de Palermo* (Buenos Aires: Instituto Amigos del Libro Argentino, 1966); El parque Tres de Febrero, *Buenos Aires nos Cuenta* 20 (1991); Diego del Pino, *Palermo un barrio porteño* (Buenos Aires: Fundación Banco de Boston, 1991); Manuel Bilbao, *Tradiciones y recuerdos de Buenos Aires* (Buenos Aires: Taller Peuser, 1934); Horacio Schiavo, Palermo de San Benito, *Cuadernos de Buenos Aires* 32 (1969).

[9] *El Nacional*, August 11, 1855.

[10] Benjamín Vicuña Mackenna, La Argentina en el año 1855, *Revista Americana de Buenos Aires* (1936).

[11] Jorge Ramos and Daniel Schavelzon, El estanque de Rosas y el baño de Manuelita en Palermo, *Revista del Instituto de Investigaciones Históricas Juan Manuel de Rosas* 28 (1992): 85-97.

[12] Fernando Aliata, Lo privado como público, Palermo de San Benito: un ejercicio de interpretación, *Revista de Arquitectura* 144 (1989): 44-53.

[13] Domingo F. Sarmiento, Arquitectura doméstica, *Revista de Ciencias, Artes y Letras* (1879), October 15.

[14] Daniel Schavelzon and Jorge Ramos, Palermo de San Benito, vindicación y rescate, *Revista de Arquitectura* 14 (1988): 30-33.

[15] Alberto de Paula, Don Felipe Senillosa, *Anales del Instituto de Arte Americano* 18 (1967): 48-85.

[16] Ramon Gutierrez, *Arquitectura colonial, teoría y praxis* (Resistencia: Instituto Argentino de Investigaciones de Historia de la Arquitectura y Urbanismo, 1980), and Arquitectura, in *Historia general del arte en la Argentina* (Buenos Aires: Academia Nacional de Bellas Artes, 1969).

[17] Aliata, Lo privado como público (1989).

[18] Mario J. Buschiazzo, *La arquitectura en la Republica Argentina 1810-1930* (Buenos Aires: published by the author, 1966).

[19] Ramon Gutierrez, *Arquitectura colonial* (1980).

[20] Jorge Ramos (1985), *Miguel Cabrera*; Ramos and Schavelzon, *Historia y arqueologia* (1989-1991).

[21] Jose Luis Busaniche, *Rosas visto por sus contemporaneos,* (Buenos Aires: EUDEBA, 1976).

[22] Domingo F. Sarmiento, *Obras Completas* X (Buenos Aires: Ediciones La Facultad, 1944): 57.

[23] *Los Debates,* April 16 (1858).

[24] Jose Garcia Enciso, *Historia del Colegio Militar de la Nacion* (Buenos Aires: Circulo Militar, 1970); Humberto Burzio, *Historia de la Escuela Naval Militar,* in Historia Naval Argentina Vol. 16 (Buenos Aires: Departamento de Estudios Historicos Navales, 1972): Colegio Militar de la Nacion, *Historia del Colegio Militar de la Nacion, edicion de su centenario* (Buenos Aires: Colegio Militar de la Nacion, 1969).

[25] Sonia Berjman, *Plazas y parques de Buenos Aires: la obra de los paisajistas franceses 1860-1960* (Buenos Aires, Fondo de Cultura Economica, 1998).

[26] We owe these notions to Diego Armús. Adrián Gorelik, *La grilla y el parque: espacio público y cultura urbana en Buenos Aires 1887-1936* (Quilmes: Universidad Nacional de Quilmes, 1998).

[27] Juan de Cominges, Palermo y el jardin zoologico hasta 1882, *Revista del Jardín Zoológico* 4 (1916): 39-82.

[28] *La Prensa,* January 26 (1899), *La Tribuna,* January 26 (1899).

[29] *La Prensa,* January 26 (1899).

[30] Author unknown, Rozas lo que queda en pie, *Caras y Caretas* 18 (1899): 23; Sobre las ruinas: La casa histórica de Don Juan Manuel. Recuerdos de un escribiente de Rosas, *La Nacion,* February 2 (1899).

[31] Schavelzon, *El Caserón de Rosas* (1986): 20.

[32] Gorelik, *La grilla y el parque* (1998).

[33] Cominges, *Palermo y el jardin zoologico hasta 1882* (1899).

[34] Domingo F. Sarmiento, *Campaña en el Ejército Grande aliado de Sud América* (Buenos Aires: Ediciones Kraft, 1957): 101-107.

[35] For the use of open spaces for official partying and the lack of restrictions to visit the place, see L.V. Mansilla (1967): 91; Carlos Ibarguren, *Juan manuel de Rosas: su vida, su drama, su tiempo* (Buenos Aires: edicion del autor): 225.

[36] *La Vanguardia,* December 7, 1901; Juan de Cominges, Palermo y el Zoológico hasta 1882, *Revista del Jardín Zoológico* 45 (1916): 39-82. For the carriages' parade-regulating plan, see Oscar Troncoso, *La modernización de Buenos Aires en 1900: archivo del intendente Adolfo J. Bullrich,* Archivo General de la ación, Buenos Aires, 2004.

[37] *La Vanguardia,* December 21 (1901).

[38] Grant provided to Sonia Berjman and Daniel Schavelzon in 1995; Osvaldo Guerrica Echevarría, *Palermo, Amigos del Lago y después,* published by the author, Buenos Aires, 2006

[39] When finally the new park was inaugurated, built under the direction of Sarmiento, the place was given a new name, which was the date in which Rosas was defeated (3 de Febrero). To many citizens this was an offensive choice, but those in power were content. It is possible that because of this unhappy choice, plus the fact that it was an imposed denomination and that the place had a name of its own from ancient times, the population has rejected it and to this day the place is referred to as Palermo.

Gardens and Cultural Change: A Pan-American Perspective

Gardens and Cultural Change: A Pan-American Perspective

Gardens and Cultural Change: A Pan-American Perspective

Gardens and Cultural Change: A Pan-American Perspective

The Small Parks in New York City and the Civilizing Process of Immigrants at the Turn of the Twentieth Century

Rachel Iannacone

When one is seated under a tree, quietly contemplating a beautiful landscape, one should not be in danger of being hit by a baseball or golf ball, or be subjected to the annoyance of boys engaged in some game, yelling close at hand (J. Olmsted 1897, 14).

It is only by degrees that the old idea of what a park should be is being revised to fit the needs of the overcrowded cities. A decade or two ago, the only thought was to preserve "bits of nature" at the outer edges of a city for those who had the leisure and the means to enjoy them….Seward Park is the best example of the new idea. It is only by looking hard that one finds the narrow border of grass which justifies the name of park. The rest is playground—to the horror and disgust, it may be added, of many worthy persons…"What a pity," say these well-meaning theorists, "to mar such a spot with unsightly swings and poles and ropes and iron bars, when these children of the poor might learn something of the beautiful if God's trees and flowers and grass were planted here" (Smith 1904, 288).

In the late nineteenth and early twentieth centuries, a public debate raged between landscape architects and reformers about the design and use of public space. Park enthusiasts and playground activists both viewed public space as a tool for social change, hoping that alterations to the built environment would improve upon the social, moral, and physical state of the citizens of the city, but they differed in their approach. Landscape architects and their supporters continued to design "bits of nature" where parkgoers could stroll or relax on a bench surrounded by trees, shrubs, and a picturesque vista. They relied on the inspirational qualities of nature and the healthful benefits of "lungs for the metropolis" (NYPA 1887) to uplift the poor, Americanize immigrants, and conquer disease. Reformers, on the other hand, sought to provide open spaces where urban dwellers could play boisterous games, run, and enjoy educational programs such as concerts and lectures. They supported direct intervention in the behaviors of the poor, developing programs that taught immigrants how to function in their new society. In essence, one group taught immigrants what they *should not* do; the other group taught immigrants what they *should* do.

The debate between park supporters and playground advocates centered on a new trend in landscape design in New York City in the 1880s: small open spaces carved out of densely built and heavily populated neighborhoods. These extensive alterations to the built environment of poor neighborhoods reflect prevalent feelings of New Yorkers during this period: a desire to compete with European and American cities; a fear that immigrants would infect millions of New Yorkers with epidemic diseases such as typhus, cholera, and tuberculosis thereby undermining efforts to recreate New York as the cultural capital of the world.

The fact that city officials hoped to compete with other cities for dominance in business and culture by building more parks is evident in numerous pamphlets printed in the 1860s through the 1890s. For example, the Commission to Select and Locate Lands for Public Parks boasted in 1894 that if the city adopted their suggestions:

> The New York of the future will be not only to the new, but to the old world as well, what London and Paris are to Europe—the great centre of capital, commerce, and enterprise, the arbiter of taste and fashion, the magnet to attract travelers from the ends of the earth (CSLLPP 1894, 50).

New York in the 1880s looked nothing like the great cities of the old world. It lacked the architecture, planning and, of course, parks. In *More Public Parks: How New York Compares with Other Cities* the New York Park Association argued, "there can be no reasonable doubt as to the urgent need for more and larger breathing spaces" (NYPA 1882, 4). Concerned that Central Park was inadequate for the size and population of New York, the New York Park Association published a table that compared the population and park acreage of New York to Philadelphia, Chicago, St. Louis and San Francisco, concluding that "to-day we are...far behind not only the great capitals of Europe, but several American cities" (5).

In addition to the desire to compete with other prestigious cities, politicians, sanitarians, and wealthy New Yorkers were desperately trying to lower high death rates. Tenement House Reform, which began in the 1860s, was the first attempt to address these concerns; however, changes to existing buildings were expensive to implement and difficult to enforce. As an alternative, reformers began to agitate for parks. For example, Dr. Timothy Newell remarked in a paper titled, *Sanitary, Physical, and Educational Advantages of Interior Open Areas in Large Cities*:

> We have all been saddened by the high death-rate in New York City during the past summer. Is not the overcrowding of the population, the want of proper ventilation of the streets, lanes, or alleys, the great primary cause of it?…The difficulties of sending the children of the poor of large cities, miles away, to a park, are not likely to be overcome;…Open squares should be brought to them, as is done in Paris (Newell 1882, 6).

Like many nineteenth-century physicians, Newell linked disease to congestion. Overcrowding and lack of ventilation were, he lamented, the cause of the high death rate in the summer of 1882. By opening spaces in the most congested districts, reformers aimed to provide "lungs" for the city. Building on the success of Central Park, leading New Yorkers proposed the creation of more large parks. In 1884, for example, the New York State Assembly passed legislation to begin purchasing land to create Van Cortlandt Park in the Bronx. While the 1,146-acre park certainly improved the city's park-to-population ratio, it did little to ameliorate health conditions of New Yorkers who lived several miles from the new park. In an address published in the *New York Tribune*, 15 May 1887, Mayor Abram S. Hewitt (1887-1888), the city's first great advocate for parks for the poor, complained that large pleasure grounds in the Bronx and Brooklyn, "are much too far away to serve the needs of that vast body of poor people....What [the poor] need are breathing places near their tenement-houses, where they can go in the evenings of hot summer days and rest in quiet, with pure air and flowers and trees and other agreeable surroundings." Hewitt initiated the first major step toward providing "pure air and flowers and trees" to the poor. On May 13, 1887, the New York State Assembly passed the Small Parks Act, which authorized the Board of Street Opening and Improvement to spend $1,000,000 annually to provide "small parks… [in] the densely populated tenement districts." In introducing the bill to the Assembly in April of 1887, Hewitt wrote that the Act was an "imperative necessity for the health, comfort, and decency of our people. The condition of some parts of the city is a reproach to civilization and humanity" ("Appeal to the Assembly" 1887).

One of the primary goals of the Small Parks Act was the elimination of disease. As such, Hewitt enlisted the newly formed Board of Health to submit reports on the health and sanitary conditions of tenement neighborhoods. Founded in 1866 in response to repeated cholera outbreaks, the Board had the single greatest influence on the location of parks during the late nineteenth century. The Health Department determined that parks should be placed in the most crowded neighborhoods because congestion was considered the major contributing factor to the spread of disease, and parks in the most crowded districts would be "used by the largest number of people" (Nagle 1887). Relying on traditional ideas of health and sickness rather than the most current scientific findings, the Board of Health and the mayor falsely pinned their hopes of fighting epidemics and disease on fresh air and open spaces. Although Louis Pasteur in France and Robert Koch in Germany had developed germ theory during the 1880s, many city officials were hesitant to embrace the notion that "bacteria, not the filth that nurtured them, was the cause of disease" (Kraut 1995, 58). For example, Dr. Timothy Newell informed the public that "the infection and diffusion of malaria or noxious emanations are arrested by trees, whose structure and canopy of foliage act in a threefold capacity: first, as a barrier to break the flow; second, as an absorbent of those emanations; third, as eliminators of nitrogen" (Newell 1882, 7-8).

Influenced by these views, the New York Board of Health focused considerable energy on cleaning up tenement neighborhoods and building open spaces for fresh air.[1] The agency oversaw the sanitary inspection of New York (although this was limited to Manhattan until the consolidation of 1898). Manhattan was divided into twenty-five districts with one inspector assigned to each. The Health Department's *Annual Report* of 1890 explained that the inspector was responsible for investigating, making reports, responding to citizen complaints, and "the frequent inspection of and report upon specific places which are likely to become dangerous to life or detrimental to health" (Health Department 1890, 17). Only weeks after the passage of the Small Parks Act, J.C. Bayles, President of the Health Department, submitted twenty-five district surveys and a map to the mayor. Drawn by Dr. John T. Nagle, Deputy Register of Vital Statistics, the map identified thirty possible park locations; more than a third (eleven) were located on the Lower East Side. Four parks were subsequently built on the exact location identified by Nagle: Mulberry Bend, Corlears Hook, East River, and Jefferson Parks.[2]

Although Hewitt championed small parks for the poor, he achieved few actual results. His greatest accomplishment was to open the gates of several V-shaped green spaces, which existed at the junction of several thoroughfares. Often less than half-an-acre in size, these squares were gated in the 1870s to protect the grass from erosion. In 1888, Hewitt directed the Parks

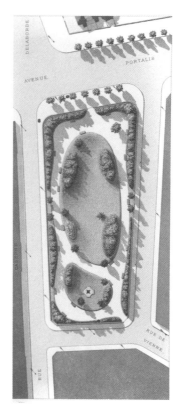

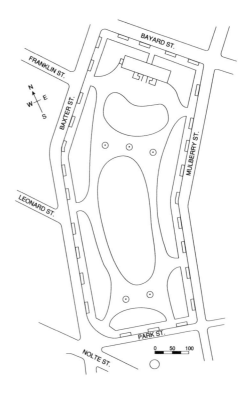

Canal Street Park, New York.

Fig. 1. Drawing of Canal Street Park, Calvert Vaux, 1892. From *Scribner's Magazine*, July 1892.
Fig. 2. Drawing of the Square Laborde, Adolphe Alphand. From *Les Promenades de Paris*, 1869.
Fig. 3. Mulberry Bend Park, c. 1897. Drawing by Katherine H. Hammond.

Department to remove the gates and asked landscape architects Calvert Vaux and Samuel Parsons, Jr. to redesign three of the squares: Canal Street Park (.3 acre), Abingdon Square (.2 acre), and Jeannette Park (.6 acre). In the decade following Hewitt's term as mayor, little progress was achieved toward building small parks for the poor. Hewitt's successors, Hugh Grant (1889-1892) and Thomas Gilroy (1893-1894), used the Parks Department as a personal and political machine for employing and enriching their friends, family, and supporters. This, coupled with the market crash of 1893, delayed the founding of the parks chosen by Hewitt, Nagle, and the Health Department. Finally, in 1897, Mayor William Strong (1895-1898) created the Small Park Advisory Committee, to which he appointed, among others, social reformer Jacob Riis and Abram Hewitt. Upon their recommendation, the Parks Department asked Calvert Vaux to design two of the parks that had been proposed in 1887: Corlears Hook Park (bounded by Jackson, Cherry, and Corlears Streets) and Mulberry Bend Park (bounded by Baxter, Park, Mulberry, and Bayard Streets). Of the five small parks Vaux designed, only one original drawing exists for Canal Street Park (Fig. 1). Most of Vaux's drawings and papers were destroyed after his death in 1895, including those of Corlears Hook and Mulberry Bend Park. Fortunately, Samuel Parsons Jr. published drawings of Abingdon Square and Jeannette Park in *Scribner's Magazine* in 1892.

Vaux's designs for small parks indicate that he was heavily influenced by Adolphe Alphand and Jean-Pierre Barillet-Deschamps' 1860s designs for small squares in Paris. Vaux's plan for Mulberry Bend Park, for example, is almost identical to Alphand's Square Laborde (Fig. 2 and Fig. 3). Vaux probably became aware of the squares of Paris during his three-month trip to Europe in 1868 when he spent much of his time "catch[ing] up on the latest developments in architecture and landscape architecture" (Kowsky 1998, 198). Evidence of his interest in the work of Alphand and Barillet-Deschamps can be found in a letter he wrote to the *New York Times* in 1878, stating that he found "the small parks and squares of Paris the perfection of artistic arrangement…The most desirable combination of the natural with the artificial…like a freely-arranged bouquet" (Vaux 1878). In addition to his own first-hand impressions, Vaux was likely influenced by William Robinson's *Parks, Promenades and Gardens of Paris* (1869) and Alphand's own publication, *Les Promenades des Paris* (1869). Vaux also may have been introduced to Alphand and Barillet-Deschamps' ideas about social and horticultural diversity through an article entitled "Squares of Paris" published in *Garden and Forest* in 1888 (Codman 1888, 267). *Garden and Forest* was a popular periodical with contributions from notable critics, historians and practitioners such as Mariana Van Rensselaer as well as Vaux's own partner, Frederick Law Olmsted. In addition to a description of Alphand's work in Paris, the author, Henry S. Codman, an associate and student of Olmsted's, included one illustration titled, "Plan of a Paris Square," that is certainly Alphand's Square Laborde.

Vaux appreciated the Parisian squares because they achieved, in a smaller form, the design ideal he espoused for larger parks, which he expressed in one book, *Villas and Cottages* (1864), and approximately a dozen articles. One basic tenet of Vaux's philosophy relied on his faith in man's love of nature and his commitment to helping the working classes. In an article he wrote in the *Horticulturist*, Vaux complained that much of American architecture relied too heavily on ornament and not enough on "high art." He proposed that by expanding the educational curriculum to include art and architecture, Americans would demand more beautiful surroundings. In his opinion, "education must be liberal and comprehensive as well as universal and cheap" (Vaux 1853, 170-171). Vaux placed responsibility for educating Americans not just on teachers, but also on architects, whom he advised to design schools and tenements. Criticizing the importance placed on private architecture for the wealthiest citizen, Vaux implored architects, artists, and writers to promote great public architecture so that "the unlettered, unthought-of common people" could be taught and uplifted (Vaux 1853, 170). He argued that public works were the most appropriate manifestation of America's republican spirit. He wrote:

> The awakening spirit of republicanism refused to acknowledge the value of art as it then existed – a tender hot-house plant, ministering to the delights of a select few – the democratic element rebelled against this idea *in toto*, and tacitly but none the less practically demanded of art to thrive in the open air in all weathers, for the benefit of all… (Vaux 1853, 170).

The parks Olmsted and Vaux designed were intended to give New Yorkers a break from their harsh urban realities, including the monotony of the grid. "We want," Olmsted wrote:

> A ground to which people may easily go after their day's work is done, and where they may stroll for an hour, seeing, hearing, and feeling nothing of the bustle and jar of the streets, where they shall in effect find the city put far away from them. We want the greatest possible contrast with the streets and the shops and rooms of the town which will be consistent with the convenience and the preservation of good order and neatness (Olmsted 1870, 80).

They hoped to uplift visitors by framing views of nature, ensuring a positive experience, and providing the visitor with an incentive to slow down and rest. Describing the need for vistas in Central Park, Vaux wrote that the "design of the terrace…should

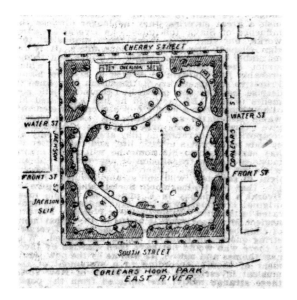

Fig. 4. Drawing of Corlears Hook Park, published in the *New York Tribune* March 31, 1895.

give good views of the water and of the Ramble, and should offer an attractive focus of interest in the landscape effects to be seen when looking over the lower Park in a southerly direction from the Ramble" (Vaux 1879). Vaux's definition of vista went beyond the simple framing of natural and urban sites and extended to people-watching. "The drive," Vaux and Olmsted wrote:

> Should…be artistically designed so as to interfere as little as possible with the views and to present all points agreeable and harmonious lines to the eye. Moreover, as it is desirable that at some point in the course of a drive through every park there should be an opportunity for those in carriages to see others and be seen by others… (Olmsted and Vaux 1866, 97).

When commissioned to design small, neighborhood parks, Vaux remained loyal to his interest in contrasting nature with the "artificial" realities of city life and belief in the importance of interesting details. With the assistance of his partner, Samuel Parsons, Jr., he designed Canal, Jeannette, and Abingdon Parks with eye-catching plantings such as those described by Parsons, "from either corner of Jeannette Park you catch long vistas between shrubs, surrounded by flashing bands of color-bedding, back to solid masses of shrubs and towering trees in the opposite diagonal corner near the Elevated Railway…and beyond, a few yards away, rolls the East River, with its varied shipping and its incessantly dancing waves" (S. Parsons 1892, 114). Vaux did not change his view of the importance of the vista when designing small parks. Instead, he framed vistas and provided many "inviting seats" in order to "tempt a man, woman or child to sit down and rest, and look about for a while…" (Vaux 1889, 141).

This was true in the first small park designed by Vaux, Corlears Hook Park. The *New York Tribune* published the only extant plan, which merely outlines the paths and lawn plantings as well as indicates the location of trees (Fig. 4). The *Tribune* also published a description, 31 March 1895:

> All of the turfed spaces are to be surrounded by shade trees…while lime trees will be planted along the outskirts of the park. These lime trees by reason of their abundant foliage will separate the park from the publicity of the surrounding streets and thus give a grateful seclusion from the busy outside world.

Shrubs and trees at the entrances sheltered parkgoers, creating an atmosphere of enclosure against the bustling life of the Lower East Side. Neighboring streets were lined with pushcarts that sold a variety of products, foods and wares, accompanied by the sounds of hawking and the odors of food. This symphony of smell, sound, and sight would have formed a stark contrast to the trees, shrubs, and flowers of the park. After entering the park, the visitor would be ushered to a bench-lined circular path along the perimeter of the park.

Corlears Hook Park was situated at the intersection of Jackson and Cherry streets, at the distant corner of the Lower

East Side of Manhattan, where it had views to the river. Vaux maximized this significant feature. Unlike large rural parks, Corlears Hook was too small for the designers to construct picturesque views at the turning point of circuitous paths. However, the views of the river enabled Vaux to create a "park-like" atmosphere (Fig. 5). The river enticed visitors to walk along the bench-lined path that circled that park toward an overlook. This vantage point afforded the parkgoers two important vistas. He could either view his densely built neighborhood from across a green lawn and blank, open space. Or, he could gaze out over the harbor toward the Manhattan Bridge or Ellis Island, his probable point of entry into America. Vaux engineered his park to inspire the user to contemplate his surroundings; the juxtaposition with the Statue of Liberty and Brooklyn Bridge was perfectly suited to Vaux's design ideas.[3]

Fig. 5. View of Corlears Hook Park from the southwest. From *Architectural Record*, July 1903.

Mulberry Bend Park has been described as "the small urban park that mattered most to Vaux" (Kowsky 1998, 308). Its creation in 1896 became a symbol of the heroic efforts and achievements of tireless advocates for the poor. If "the Bend," as it was called, could become an oasis within the slums of New York, then parks truly could improve any neighborhood. The earliest surviving drawing of Mulberry Bend Park is a dirty line drawing probably executed by a surveyor for the Parks Department in 1911 (See Fig. 3). Several early photographs and descriptions confirm that the drawing fairly represents the original lawn plantings and paths as Vaux designed them (Fig. 6). Vaux employed the same design features as he did in Corlears Hook Park in the smaller and more irregularly shaped Mulberry Bend Park including a central greensward, paths that circled the perimeter, and a kidney-shaped lawn in front of a pavilion. The curved paths contrasted with the strict geometry of the streets of New York. Along with the *Tribune's* description, 9 May 1897, that "the grass in these public places is not to be trodden on by the feet of the residents of the vicinity," photographs show that all the lawns were lined with benches that barred visitors from walking or playing on the grass. The park was not meant for active recreation; instead, immigrants were drawn to the park and barred from stepping foot on the inviting grass.

While providing breathing space for the poor and ventilating the city, Vaux's parks also exerted indirect methods of social control to uplift and civilize immigrants. They were, first, models of a better life. George Burnap, a well-known park enthusiast, argued that a park that is "a grade higher than that to which they are accustomed [will] encourage a desire in them for something better" (Burnap 1916, 102-104). Second, the small parks aimed to draw the surrounding population out of their dwellings and into a public sphere where they could be policed, disciplined, and surveyed. Nineteenth-century New Yorkers were anxious about the activities of immigrants behind closed doors, as evidenced by the home inspections and detailed reports

Fig. 6. View of Mulberry Bend Park from the south. From *Architectural Record*, July 1903.

conducted by the health department. In addition to investigating the private habits of the poor, city leaders sought to draw immigrants into the light. Park benches, for example, were placed "with an eye…to the loafers of the district, who can thus be all watched at once" (Lee 1902, 175). Small parks were also the perfect stage on which to display immigrants to the wider public who could easily watch the specimen in his own surroundings. Rather than having to read about the "hot-headed Italian" or view photographs of the "pagan Chinaman," New Yorkers could walk past the park and see firsthand the "poor wretches" of the Lower East Side.[4]

Although the description of Corlears Hook Park stated that it was meant to have full trees around the perimeter "to separate the park from the publicity of the surrounding streets and thus giving a grateful seclusion from the busy outside world," all photographs of Corlears Hook and Mulberry Bend Parks through 1915 show that trees and shrubs never grew to such a size that they blocked views into or out of the parks (Fig. 5). Without this foliage to block the gaze, any outsider could look into the park and judge the progress of individual immigrants toward assimilation and civilization. Because it existed in the neighborhoods where the health inspectors identified the greatest problems, even those immigrants who were uninterested in enjoying nature had the benefits of a park. Strolling, resting, and contemplating were introduced as model behavior to all who lived in the neighborhood. While the parks afforded outsiders, such as reformers and settlement workers, the opportunity to monitor immigrants, neighbors were also unknowingly recruited to supervise each other. With the park so close to surrounding buildings, the tenants with windows upon the park became monitors of behavior. Looking out of their windows, even without intent, their gaze was implicit in an act of surveillance. The constant presence of viewers deterred behaviors that parkgoers would not wish to commit in public.[5]

The creation of Corlears Hook and Mulberry Bend Parks was a monumental step. The city government, supported by state funds, had built two green oases amidst two dilapidated, overcrowded, and dangerous neighborhoods on the Lower East Side. Nevertheless, many liberals and reformers looked at these parks and saw an old-fashioned, failed attempt on the part of effete intellectuals and snobs to reform the poor by pushing upper-class notions of leisure on the poor, and failing entirely to accommodate the needs of the community to exercise and have fun. Central Park provided many opportunities to wealthy New Yorkers to exercise; they could play tennis, horse ride, and ice skate. In the new small parks, poor New Yorkers were warned to "keep of the grass." They were forbidden to play bocce, drink alcohol, or play music. The city had yet to build a park *for* the poor. That was to change.

At the same time that Calvert Vaux was imagining ways to miniaturize the picturesque and finding inspiration in the small parks of Europe, a national recreation movement was gaining power and influence in the United States. Among others, Luther Halsey Gulick and Joseph Lee (responsible for founding the Camp Fire Girls and the National Recreation Organization respectively), developed pedagogical methods and theories regarding the benefits of play and team sports. They lectured and wrote about the need for American cities to organize recreational programs, team sports, and intra-city competitions and build parks designed to accommodate such activities. Play, they argued, was an important factor in changing behavior and making a better America:

> In addition to receiving the physical benefits that come from wholesome outdoor exercise and the intellectual benefits that come from useful constructive work, the little children playing on the sand pile learn fundamental lessons in mutual rights….[B]y having to play by the rules of the game…they learn that the social unit is larger than the individual unit, that individual victory is not as sweet as the victory of the team, and that the most perfect self-realization is won by the most perfect sinking of one's self in the welfare of the larger unity—the team (Gulick 1907, 481).

Play had the power to create better workers, decrease crime, inspire civic pride, and encourage domestic order, hygiene, and patriotism. The necessity for public playgrounds, rested in their ability to teach "the lesson of personal discipline and restraint, which orderly play makes mandatory" (Harder 1898, 2).

The National Recreation Movement inspired local educators and activists to agitate for playgrounds instead of parks. In New York City, public school teachers were responsible for many changes in park design and policy. In the late nineteenth century, public education attracted reformers and activists who believed that education was the only path to a better future for New York. In 1888, the Education and Health Departments collaborated with the Parks Department to begin offering free lectures to the working people of the city (Education Department 1904, 7). New York citizens from the poor and immigrant classes, as well as the middle class, gathered in parks to listen to lectures on a wide range of topics. While many speakers addressed health, hygiene, and citizenship, others spoke about "Italian Opera," "Italian Folk Songs," "King Lear," and "The Forms and Motions of the Earth" (Education Department 1903/1904). Over the years, the program expanded, and lectures were given in Yiddish and Italian as well as English. While some of these foreign-language lectures focused on art and science, most "related chiefly to American History and Biography, American Institutions, the rights and duties of American Citizenship, and also the principles of Sanitation and Hygiene" (Paulding 1899, 1). Vaux and Parsons' small parks were now used as outdoor schoolrooms. The success of these programs encouraged the Parks Department to allocate more funds to programming, necessitating alterations and fostering a new aesthetic for public space. For example, in 1906, the central lawn of Mulberry Bend Park was converted into a gymnasium ground that could also serve as a meeting space and lecture ground.

A program, initiated in 1898, which staged free concerts in public parks, similarly demonstrates the ways that educational reformers were effecting change to public space policy by slowly adapting public spaces for educational purposes. Music in the parks was intended to introduce "high-quality music education for the immigrant, ethnic, and working poor, exposure to uplifting classical concert performances, and efforts to supply visitors with affordable alternatives to commercial musical amusements [that] could dramatically enhance the welfare of the urban population and promote civic engagement"

Fig. 7. Illustration of a musical concert in Tompkins Square Park, 1981. From *Harpers Weekly*, 12 September 1981.
Fig. 8. Illustration of a musical concert in Tompkins Square Park, 1901. From *Century Magazine*, August 1901.

(Vaillant 2003, 94). Rather than demanding the creation of new parks entirely devoted to education, these reformers merely asked to use public space temporarily. The first summer, the city hosted thirty-seven concerts: thirteen in East River Park, twelve in Corlears Hook Park, and twelve in Mulberry Bend Park (Parks Department 1898, 23). Two years later, the program had more than doubled to ninety-three concerts: thirty in Central Park, twelve in Corlears Hook, Tompkins Square, Mulberry Bend, Hudson and Seward Parks and thirteen in East River Park (Parks Department 1902, 11). In another two years, the program had doubled again with a total of 180 concerts: thirty in Central Park, twelve in Madison Square, Corlears Hook, East River, Battery Park, Seward, Mount Morris, Tompkins, Washington Square, Abingdon Square, Hudson, Mulberry Bend, Morningside and ten in Hamilton Fish (Parks Department 1902, 43). The concerts were so popular that by 1904, the Department needed additional funds; demonstrating its approval, the Board of Estimates and Apportionment awarded the Parks Department $10,000 to expand the musical program (Pallas 1904).

Since the parks were not designed to accommodate large audiences, the department invented different approaches to stage these concerts. The use of the parks for this purpose altered the way that the public and park officials viewed landscape. Initially, audience members were barred from sitting on the grass. As represented in drawings and photographs of Tompkins Square Park in 1891, the audience strolled through the park while the band played from the gazebo (Fig. 7). By 1901, a second illustration of a concert in Tompkins Square Park shows people sitting on benches surrounding the gazebo (Fig. 8). The scene was described in the *Evening Post*: "On the lawns that stretch in front of the stand, and on the sidewalks on either side, thousands of early comers take their seats in the long rows of park benches and camp chairs placed there for them. Even before the musicians arrive, standing room behind the last rows begins to be sought" (*Evening Post* 1901, 317). By 1906, even the lawns in Central Park served as seating areas for children and mothers to enjoy the "civilizing influence" of Municipal Music. This was certainly a far cry from "Keep of the Grass" signs, which were standard in 1895 when Corlears Hook Park opened.

One of the most important and interesting programs developed in this period was the Farm School Program, which was the creation of a strong and dedicated educational reformer, Fannie Griscom Parson.[6] Her career with the Department of Parks reflects the changes that were occurring not only in the municipal organization of New York City, but throughout the nation, where educators, amateurs, and activists began to dominate parks administration. With no training in landscape or gardening, she acted as the Director of the Farm Schools from 1902 to 1919. In that time, she opened five schools: DeWitt Clinton (1902), Thomas Jefferson (1908), Corlears Hook (1912), Isham Park (1913) and Seward Park (1914). Parsons opened the first farm school in 1902 in conjunction with the Outdoor Recreation League, which had negotiated with the Department of Education to co-sponsor a kindergarten and playground on property that had been condemned by the city to build a park, but had not yet been developed. In 1905, the Parks Department rebuilt the park, incorporating the farm school in the new design. Her farm school attracted hundreds of visitors from all over the United States and even from Europe. More importantly, she was an excellent spokesperson for her experimental "patches," publishing reports and newsletters with photographs and accounts of her triumphs.

Parsons was a skilled reformer, well versed in the most up-to-date educational philosophies. Her work was closely linked with the educational philosophies of Luther Halsey Gulick, who, according to a list of visitors published in the *Annual Reports* of 1904 and 1905, was a frequent visitor to the farm schools. Gulick urged educators to incorporate physical activity into their lessons and balance instruction with experiential learning. The farm schools became a prominent model showcasing the positive benefits of Gulick's ideas. Parsons' guiding principles incorporated both traditional educational methods such as lecturing and recitation, as well as experimental methods that encouraged students to work independently and collaboratively. On the one hand, she valued discipline and order: "As the whistle sounded each fell to work most dexterously, raking toward the center path where stood others with wheelbarrows ready to gather up the piles, and in a few minutes…our Farm was a beautiful picture with its symmetrical paths and plots left in order for the night" (F. Parsons 1903a, 72). On the other hand, she gave students a great deal of freedom to experience nature and to create their own learning plan. Students were given their own plot to tend if they agreed to contribute to the overall maintenance of the farm school and follow the rules. In this way, she balanced personal ownership with community responsibility:

> By having children lay a strip of sod about the flower beds and the making of a… miniature lawn, and being expected to take care of this and keep it in such condition that it will not mar the beauty of the garden they gradually learn, as in no other way, why the lawns outside the garden, maintained by the City, must be taken care of and protected. The ownership of an individual plot and confining that owner's care to that one plot, in short time develops selfishness in the children. This is overcome by requiring from each and all a general care of this whole garden, such as paths, decorative flower beds and grass, so uniting individual ownership with a responsibility for the appearance of the whole, making a foundation for good citizenship (Parks Department 1910, 51).

Fig. 9. DeWitt Clinton Farm School looking toward Fifty-Second Street. Hudson River is to the left. From Department of Parks, *Annual Report*, 1905.
Fig. 10. Thomas Jefferson Farm School looking toward the East River. From Parks Department, *Annual Report*, 1902.

While the concept of public parks had been established in New York over fifty years earlier, with the planning and execution of Central Park, landscape philosophers such as Andrew Jackson Downing and Frederick Law Olmsted never articulated this definition of private ownership of public space. Instead, they viewed the public park as a gift, bestowed upon the citizens for their enjoyment and edification. In Parsons' new approach to public space, the park became the property (and responsibility) of its users. The farm, she argued, was "truly their own" (F. Parsons 1903a, 68).

Parsons' farm schools also helped redefine the role of women in public, drawing attention to the important contribution of women both in the professional and domestic spheres. First, the farm school showcased the work of female educators by placing them on a stage where they could be watched both by hundreds of neighbors and visitors. In photographs, female teachers are surrounded by small children as they conduct their professional business in public (Fig. 9). In this public role, teachers also functioned as mentors and models of behavior for poor and middle-class girls and women, demonstrating the benefits of education and the professional possibilities available to women in America.

The farm schools also highlighted the domestic work of women and mothers. First, Parsons constructed a model home in each farm school, where she taught the wifely duties of ironing and washing. In this way, women's work was brought into the public sphere where it could be compared to the commercial work of men, whose businesses, shops, and carts lined adjacent streets. Second, Parsons viewed the role of female educators as an extension of motherhood. Describing the development of her farm school curriculum, she wrote, "Seeing the confusion existing on every hand, I simply went out to live with the thousands, as I had lived with my own seven [children]" (F. Parsons 1903b, 223). She moved mothering from the private realm of the home to the public sphere of the park and thereby claimed public space as a domestic arena.

Fannie Parsons' farm schools unintentionally altered the American perception of public space and landscape architecture. Unlike the parks designed by Calvert Vaux, the furrows and garden plots of Parsons' school extended the urban grid inside the park; in addition, where Vaux tried to draw the viewer's eye to vistas and landmarks outside the park, Parsons' school drew attention to activities occurring within the park. The teachers, children, and plants became the objects of the gaze rather than monuments and bridges. The image of children kneeling to plant seeds against the backdrop of warehouses and factories challenged viewers to wonder how these children spent their days. By conducting their classes in the open air, the classroom became a kind of theater. The farm schools drew attention to the hundreds of children involved in the program, including immigrants and handicapped children. Unlike most handicapped children who were often taken to hospitals, rendering them invisible to the public, these children played and learned in the heart of the densest neighborhoods. Adding to the visual interest, the plots changed with the seasons, connecting parkgoers to the cycle of nature. At times, the ground was newly tilled and planted and appeared orderly, with each plot clearly labeled and delineated. Later in the summer, as students tended their patches, the dry ground was miraculously transformed into a fertile and abundant harvest with plants that towered over the small children (Fig. 10).

At Fannie Griscom Parsons' farm schools, children were no longer warned to "keep off the grass." Instead, they were urged to get their hands and toes dirty and dig up public property. She encouraged Americans to change the ways they viewed women's work, citizenship, education, and public space. The concert, lecture, and farm school represents a continuation of the democratization of our cities and the politicization of public space.

Initially, the Parks Department made temporary concessions in order to accommodate increasingly popular programs. As the century drew to a close, private activist organizations influenced the Parks Department to implement permanent facilities for educational programs and active recreation. City officials were initially hesitant to abandon trees, shrubbery, and grass entirely. First, they built several park-playgrounds, a transitional type of public space that accommodated philosophies from both sides of the fence. Seward Park, which is considered the first municipally-sponsored playground in America, is in fact a park-playground. Its design resulted from a yearlong debate between Charles Stover, a dedicated social reformer, and Samuel Parsons, Jr., landscape architect for the Parks Department and devoted protégé of Calvert Vaux.

Although Charles Stover lacked any experience of landscape architecture, horticulture, or gardening, his advocacy for playgrounds in every neighborhood of the city had an enormous effect on the design of public space in the twentieth century. Stover founded the Outdoor Recreation League in 1890 (originally called the Lower East Side Recreation Society).[7] Unlike other organizations devoted to the playground movement, the work of the Outdoor Recreation League was overtly political. Stover convinced the Parks Department to open privately run playgrounds on city owned property. He was determined not only to provide playgrounds to the poor, but also to "arouse public interest, through means of the press, personal influence, public conferences, etc., in the need for playgrounds for young people and increased opportunities for healthful recreation for the people generally" (ORL *Minutes* 1898). He did not view his work as charitable, but political, insisting that "this League is not a charity; it seeks rather to be the organ of private activity in a certain public work…." (ORL 1898). He sought both to shift the responsibility of social welfare from private charities to public engines and to give private citizens a voice in the design of public space.

The history of Charles Stover's greatest victory, the founding of Seward Park, demonstrates the growing influence of social advocates on the design and programming of public space at the turn of the century. In 1887, Abram Hewitt's Small Park Advisory Committee (SPAC) selected the property (2.651 acres) bounded by Hester, Suffolk, Jefferson, Canal, Essex and East

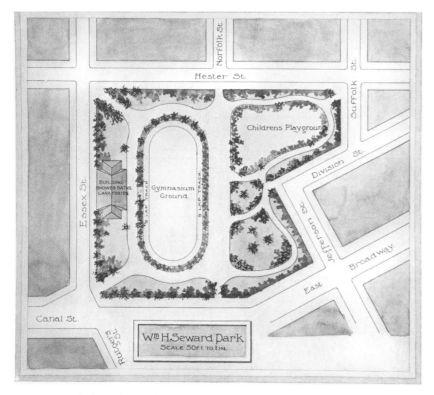

Fig. 11. Final Plan of Seward Park, Samuel Parsons, Jr. 1902. From Parks Department, *Annual Report*, 1902.

Broadway as the future site of Seward Park (Ballard 1887). After ten years of inaction, the city finally purchased the property on June 22, 1897. Although the city razed the property in 1897, they made no preparations to build a park. Nearly one year after the demolition of hundreds of people's homes and businesses,[8] the Outdoor Recreation League published and circulated *An Appeal* (June 17, 1898) in which they wrote: "Manhattan Island contains no more desolate and disgraceful spot than the so-called small park bounded by East Broadway, Essex, Suffolk and Hester streets. The houses have been torn down, leaving behind unsightly ruins, in which is dumped refuse, that now festers in the summer sun." (ORL 1898, 3) Alleging mismanagement, Stover persuaded the Parks Department to allow the newly formed Outdoor Recreation League "to erect an open

air gymnasium" (ORL 1899, 3). Simultaneously, he began lobbying for a permanent design that combined lawns and paths with areas for recreation (ORL *Minutes* 1899). While no drawings remain, minutes of the Park Board indicate that Samuel Parsons, Jr., landscape architect for the Parks Department, was asked to design the new park at the same time that Stover and the Outdoor Recreation League drew up their own plans. Still trying to abandon the project, the parks commissioner threatened to turn the property over to the Board of Education. Stover refused to relinquish control of the park, forcing the department to continue negotiating a final plan (ORL *Minutes* 1900).

In October, the Board of Estimate and Apportionment approved Samuel Parsons' design, which Commissioner Clausen described as "a small park in the natural style with lawns and shrubberies covering as large an area as possible." Stover was outraged, arguing that the layout showed "no regard for our plans…These plans provided nothing but an old-style park of asphalt paths and lawns, with the regulation 'keep-off-the-grass' signs." He collected 50,000 signatures on a petition that demanded that at least one-third of the park be reserved for recreation and play. The Parks Department yielded and the new designs were rescinded. By the end of the year, the Park Board, without consulting the Outdoor Recreation League, presented another plan, which included a gymnasium and playground. Stover was implacable and argued: "these plans conformed to the letter of the law, but not to our notion of the proper apportionment of the park space," and in January 1901, the Board of Estimate and Apportionment rejected the second plan as well (ORL *Minutes* 1901).

A third set of plans was presented at a public meeting in the middle of January 1901 where, according to Stover, the Parks Department finally showed a desire to work with the League. Mayor Robert Van Wyck (1898-1901) bowed to Stover's pressure and "moved that the plans as presented by the Park Department be rescinded and that the Park Department be requested to make new plans setting aside a substantial part of the park for a playground." In addition, on January 19, 1901, The *New York Tribune* reported that Van Wyck was, "strongly in favor of small parks in the city, but a park like this should almost wholly be given up in a playground. I really think it would be better to have the whole park a playground." The final plans, adopted on December 30, 1901, included an enclosed

Fig. 12. Bird's Eye View of Seward Park. From *Munsey's Magazine*, 1904.

playground, gym and running track, 20,600 square feet of asphalt, 28,000 square feet of sod, a pavilion, a gymnasium, a playground, and sand piles for small children on the Suffolk Street side, lawns, and paths (ORL *Minutes* 1902).

Parsons' final design was remarkable in its attempt to accommodate play equipment (Fig. 11). Officially opened on October 17, 1903, Seward Park became famous as the first municipally funded playground in the United States. Newspapers and national magazines published articles and photographs of the state-of-the-art equipment. *Munsey's Magazine* ran a photograph of Seward Park in 1904 with the caption, "it is claimed that this public playground…is the best-equipped in the world" (Smith 1904, 287). However, very little had actually changed (Fig. 12) (Smith, 1904). Parkgoers were still barred from the grass by rows of benches. The plan indicates the "gymnasium ground" and "children's playground," it also calls for plants and shrubs throughout. When looking at this plan, one wonders how much it differs from the first design that Stover criticized as an "old style" park with "regulation 'keep-of-the-grass' signs."

The last phase of the great picturesque movement of Alphand, Nash, and Olmsted came to an end on the lower east side of New York with the design of Seward Park. The rivalry of ideas about the form and function of public space was exemplified by the personal battle between Samuel Parsons, Jr. and Charles Stover. It is ironic that Parsons, an artist opposed to the idea of play and recreation in parks, designed the first publicly funded playground in America. By the end of his career with the city, the parks department was less an agency of landscape design within the large urban metropolis, and more an engine of public welfare whose agenda focused more on shaping behavior through educational programming than on landscape architecture and artistry. Only a few years after Seward Park opened, the city abandoned the park-playground in favor of the playground. In 1906, St. Gabriel's Park opened. Paved throughout with not a tree or blade of grass in sight, it was the first of many play spaces built exclusively for team-based sports and exercise classes. Another event marked the diminishing role of design in public parks. In 1908, Charles Stover was appointed New York City Parks Commissioner, and in 1911, he fired Samuel Parsons.

Bibliography

"Appeal to the Assembly; A Petition to the State for Justice to the City." *New York Times* 21 April 1887.

Alphand, Adolphe. *Les Promenades de Paris*. 1873. Reprint. Princeton, NJ: Princeton Architectural Press, 1984.

Ballard, William to Walter D.F. Day. 23 May 1887, Mayor's Papers. New York City Department of Records and Information Services.

Brace, Charles Loring. *The Dangerous Classes of New York*. (New York: Wynkoop & Hallenbeck, 1872).

Burnap, George. *Parks, Their Design, Equipment and Use*. Philadelphia: Lippincott, 1916.

Codman, Henry S. "The Squares of Paris." *Garden and Forest* 1 (August 1, 1888): 267.

Commission to Select and Locate Lands for Public Parks. Report to the New York Legislature. New York: Martin B. Brown Company, 1884.

Education Department. "Education for Adults. The History of the Free Lecture System of the City of New York.," 1904.

---. *Report of the Free Lectures to the People*. 1903-1904.

Evening Post quoted in "Democratization of Music." *Current Literature* 49, 3: (September 1901): 317.

Gutman, Marta. "On the Ground in Oakland: Women and Institution Building in an Industrial City." Ph.D. diss., University of California, Berkeley, 2000.

Harder, F. "The Necessity for Public Playgrounds." *Advocate* 1, no. 2 (October 1898): 2.

Health Department. *Annual Report 1890*. New York: Martin B. Brown Company, 1891.

Kowsky, Francis R. *Country, Park & City; The Architecture and Life of Calvert Vaux*. New York: Oxford University Press, 1998.

Kraut, Alan M. *Silent Travelers: Germs, Genes, and the 'Immigrant Menace'*. Baltimore: Johns Hopkins University Press, 1995.

Lee, Joseph. *Constructive and Preventive Philanthropy*. New York: MacMillan Co., 1902.

Gulick, Luther H. "Play and Democracy." *Charities* 18, no 18 (August 3, 1907): 481-486.

Morris, Morris to Walter D.F. Day, MD, Sanitary Superintendent, May 24, 1887, Mayors Papers, New York Municipal Archives.

Nagle, John T. to W. Det. Day, MD of the Health Department, Sanitary Bureau, 25 May 1887, Mayor's Papers. New York City Department of Records and Information Services.

New York Park Association. *More Public Parks: How New York Compares with Other Cities. Lungs for the Metropolis. The Financial and Sanitary Aspects of the Question*. New York: New York Park Association, 1882.

Newell, Timothy, M.D. *Sanitary, Physical, and Educational Advantages of Interior Open Areas in Large Cities*. Boston: Rockwell and Churchill, 1882.

Olmsted, Frederick Law and Calvert Vaux. "Report of the Landscape Architect," *Annual Report of the Commissioners of Prospect Park*. (1866).

Olmsted, Frederick Law. "Public Parks and the Enlargement of Towns," American Social Science Association (Cambridge, MA: Riverside Press, 1870) reprinted in *Civilizing American Cities Writing on City Landscapes*. Edited by S. B. Sutton. Cambridge, MA: MIT Press, 1997.

Olmsted, John C. "The True Purpose of a Large Public Park." in *Report of the American Park and Outdoor Art Association* 1 (1897).

Outdoor Recreation League. "An Appeal." June 17, 1898, The Papers of the University Settlement Society of New York City.

---. *Advocate* 13 April 1899.

---. *Advocate* October 1898.

---. *Minutes*. The Papers of the University Settlement Society of New York City, State Historical Society of Wisconsin, Madison.

Pallas, John. Letter to Board of Estimate and Apportionment, 10 August 1904, Mayor's Papers, New York City Department of Records and Information Services.

Parks Department. *Annual Report 1898*. New York: Martin B. Brown Company, 1899.

---. *Annual Report 1902*. New York: Martin B. Brown Company, 1903.

---. *Annual Report 1910*. New York: Martin B. Brown Company, 1911.

Parsons, Fannie Griscom. 1903a. "The First Children's Farm," *Outlook* 74 (May 2, 1903): 67-72.

---. 1903b. "The Second Children's Farm School in New York City." *Charities* 11, no 10 (5 Sep 1903): 220-223.

Parsons, Samuel, Jr. "Evolution of a City Square." *Scribner's Magazine* 12 (July 1892): 107-116.

Paulding, James Kirk. *Charles B. Stover: His Life and Personality*. New York: International Press, 1938.

-----. "The Outdoor Recreation League." *Charities* 3, no. 2 (August 12, 1899).

Pentecost, George F. Jr. "City Gardens." *Architectural Record* 14 (July 1903).

Riis, Jacob. *How the Other Half Lives: Studies Among the Tenements of New York*. New York: Scribner's Sons, 1890.

Robinson William. *Parks, Promenades and Gardens of Paris,* 1869.

Smith, Bertha H. "City Playgrounds: How the Old-Fashioned Idea of a Park has been Modified." *Munsey's Magazine* 31, no.2 (May 1904): 287-294.

"Tompkins Square; Popular Concert," *Harper's Weekly* (September 12, 1891).

Vaillant, Derek. *Sounds of Reform: Progressivism and Music in Chicago, 1873-1935.* Chapel Hill: University of North Carolina, 2003.

Van Rensselaer, Mrs. Schuyler. "Midsummer in New York," *Century* 42: (August 1901).

Vaux, Calvert. "American Architecture." *The Horticulturalist* 8 (April 1853): 168-172.

---. "City Zoological Garden." *New York Times*, 3 March 1878.

---. "A Plea for the Artistic Unity of Central Park," *New York Times*, 27 August 1879.

---. "Street Planning in Relation to Architectural Design." *Proceedings of the Architectural League of New York* (1889): 135-146.

---. *Villas and Cottages.* New York: Harpers and Brothers, 1864.

Notes

[1] The Health Department initiated programs to provide discounted and free medical care in the 1880s; however, these were combined with substantial efforts to improve hygiene in the homes of immigrants and the poor.

[2] Of the remaining twenty-six, seven significant small parks (John Jay, DeWitt Clinton, Hamilton Fish, Chelsea, Seward, Hudson, and St. Gabriel's) were built within four blocks of suggested locations. It is a testament to the power of plans as well as to the influence of the Health Department on urban planning during this period that Nagle's oil-pencil marks and the hand-written reports of twenty-five inspectors exerted an influence on the siting of new open-spaces for decades to follow.

[3] President Grover Cleveland dedicated the Statue of Liberty on October 28, 1886.

[4] Terms like these can be found throughout contemporary literature (Riis 1890 and Brace 1872).

[5] A disparity existed between the behaviors that neighbors might view as inappropriate and those that the city wished to curb. This research explores prescribed behaviors, not the actual activities of immigrants in parks.

[6] Fannie Griscom Parsons (1850-1923), a descendent of Charles Willson Peale, was influenced by her reform-minded grandfather, John Griscom (1774-1852) and father, John Hoskins Griscom (1809-1874). Her grandfather founded the New York High School, an experimental monitorial school, which relied on pupils to "monitor" the school themselves as active participants in their own education. He also wrote several books outlining his theories of educational reform. Following this tradition of social activism, her father was a leader in sanitary reform; his The *Sanitary Condition of the Laboring Class of New York, with Suggestions for its Improvement* (1845) exposed the deplorable conditions of the city of New York and inspired tenement reform legislation. As a physician for the New York Hospital and New York Dispensary and as an inspector and later the Director of the Board of Health, John Hoskins Griscom surveyed the dark halls and basements of New York's tenements. Fannie was especially influenced by her father's revolutionary approach to diagnosing the sanitary and health conditions. Unlike most other inspectors and physicians, Griscom refused to blame the poor for their pitiable circumstances. He recommended parks. Along with William Cullen Bryant, George W. Curtis and A.J. Downing, he pressured New York's leaders to build more parks.

[7] The history of the Outdoor Recreation League has only been explored in one published account (Paulding 1938). Although Paulding's account is useful, it is largely a eulogy for the work and life of his longtime friend. My understanding of the work and agenda of the League derived mainly from three sources. *Charities Magazine* published frequent accounts of the progress of the Outdoor Recreation League, including requests for money and volunteers. The Charity Organization Society of New York (COSNY) began publishing *Charities Magazine*, the "Official Organ of the Charity Organization Society of the City of New York" in December 1897 as a monthly magazine (within one year the magazine became a weekly) to inform donors, workers, reformers, and city employees of various charitable associations and their work. Secondly, the League published four volumes of the *Advocate* from August 1898 to March 1900. Lastly, the records and Minutes of the Outdoor Recreation League exist as part of the Papers of the University Settlement Society of New York City at the State Historical Society of Wisconsin, Madison.

[8] Articles in the *New York Tribune* indicate that two hundred storekeepers met to complain about the new park. Owners received notification on July 22 that they would have to vacate the property and that demolition would begin on August 20, causing many to lose money and clients. Sale of the houses was postponed two weeks.

Gardens and Cultural Change: A Pan-American Perspective

Gardens and Cultural Change: A Pan-American Perspective

Gardens and Cultural Change: A Pan-American Perspective

Gardens and Cultural Change: A Pan-American Perspective

Contributors

Catherine Benoît is a Professor of Anthropology at Connecticut College. She received her Ph.D. in social and cultural anthropology from the Ecole des Hautes Etudes en Sciences Sociales in Paris. Her research interests on landscape reflect her interdisciplinary training in literature, archaeology, and social and cultural anthropology. As a medievalist archeologist she has explored the transformation of landscape in the French region of La Dombes as reflecting agricultural and social changes in XIII-XVth medieval Europe. Then moving to the field of Caribbean studies, Professor Benoît's research has focused on the study of space and gardens in relation to the definition of the body and the self.

In recent years, Professor Benoît has been a fellow in Gardens and Landscape Studies at Dumbarton Oaks and at the Gilder Lehrman Center for the Study of Slavery, Resistance and Abolition at Yale University to conduct research about the history of gardens among African Americans in the Caribbean and the U.S. In 2000 she published "Corps, jardins, mémoires: Anthropologie du corps et de l'espace à la Guadeloupe" (CNRS Editions/MSH) and is currently working on a book that explores the role of space and gardens in the development of African American and Caribbean identities.

Sonia Berjman holds a Ph.D. in the History of Art from the Universidad de Buenos Aires and a Doctorat in Histoire del'Art from the Université de la Sorbonne. Her post-doctoral studies were held at Dumbarton Oaks Library in Washington D.C. (Trustees for Harvard University). Her field of study is urban history specializing in public space and landscape history, having written around 100 publications on those subjects. She has conducted research for some of the most important organizations in Argentina and abroad, and has been a lecturer throughout Latin America and Europe. Dr. Berjman has been a researcher at the Argentina National Council of Research and the Universidad de Buenos Aires, graduate professor at several Argentinean universities, and Director to the Master on Environment, Landscape and Heritage (Universidad Nacional del Nordeste, Argentina).

She earned several awards, including the "Buenos Aires City Historian" by the City Council and the "Gardens at risk" by Dumbarton Oaks. She is a member of the following magazine boards: Paisagem e Ambiente (Universidade de Sao Paulo, Brazil) and Revista de Arquitectura (Universidad Católica de Colombia). She is currently Vice President to the ICOMOS-IFLA Cultural Landscapes Committee and member of several professional organizations in her country and abroad, and a former member of the Landscape Senior Fellow Committee at Dumbarton Oaks Landscape Studies.

Michel Conan is a sociologist. His research has focused on processes of architectural design, on evaluation of public programs, and on the cultural history of garden design. He is presently Director of Garden and Landscape Studies and Curator of the Contemporary Design Collections at Dumbarton Oaks. He has edited nine Dumbarton Oaks volumes (www. Doaks. org). His most recent publications are: *The Quarries of Crazannes by Bernard Lassus, An Essay Analyzing the Creation of a Landscape,* Washington D.C. Spacemaker Press, 2004; a reprint with an introductory study of Gabriel Thouin*, Les Plans raisonnés de toutes les espèces de jardins*, Paris: Bibliothèque des Introuvables, 2004; and *Essais de Poétique des Jardins*, Firenze: Daniele Olschki, 2004.

Rachel Iannacone received her Ph.D. from the History of Art Department at the University of Pennsylvania, where she was trained as a historian of 18th, 19th and 20th century architecture and landscape architecture. She is currently a visiting assistant professor at the School of Architecture at the University of Minnesota. Her research interests focus on the study of the built environment within its historical and social context and the ways architectural design and urban planning reflect the intricate networks of public life. Professor Iannacone is working on a book that explores the Small Parks Movement in New York City, placing it in a national context. She is exploring how these parks were used and, in turn, adapted by their users. She recently contributed two essays, "Central Park," and "Neighborhood Parks and Playgrounds," to *Robert Moses and the Transformation of New York* (Rizzoli 2007), edited by Hilary Ballon and Kenneth Jackson.

Saúl Alcántara Onofre is a Professor and architect at the Metropolitan Autonomous University-Azcapotzalco, Mexico. He received a degree in landscape architecture from the Universitá degli Studi di Genova, Italy, and a design doctor from the Metropolitan Autonomus University-Azcapotzalco, Mexico. He is a member of the National Researchers System of Mexico, an active member of the International Scientific Committee of Cultural Landscapes ICOMOS-IFLA, and member of the Architecture National Academy.

Jeffrey Quilter is an archaeologist with research interests in Peru and southern Central America. He was the Director of Pre-Columbian studies at Dumbarton Oaks from 1995 to 2005, and currently is Deputy Director for Curatorial Affairs and Curator for Intermediate Area Archaeology at the Peabody Museum, Harvard University. He has edited numerous Symposium volumes at Dumbarton Oaks and is the author of three books the most recent of which is *Treasures of the Andes* (Duncan Baird, 2005). Among his research interests are the nature, production, and reception of images in prehistoric societies, especially those of ancient America and the relationships between art, politics, and religion as interpreted from them.

Daniel Schavelzon, born in Buenos Aires, is an architect (UBA) and has obtained a Master's degree in Monument Restoration (UNAM, México), and a Ph.D. in Prehispanic Architecture (UNAM, México). He has founded and ever since conducted the Center for Urban Archaeology (FADU, University of Buenos Aires), the Area of Urban Archaeology for the City Government of Buenos Aires, and the Foundational Area of Mendoza, among others. He has encouraged the creation of work teams devoted to research in both his own country and Latin America. He is presently Chief Researcher at the National Council of Science and Technology. His major subjects of interest are historic archaeology in urban settings, conservation of cultural heritage, cultural policies and illegal trafficking of art. He is the founder of the National Congresses of Historic Archaeology. In recent years he has published: *Arqueología Histórica de Buenos Aires* (4 vol., 1991-1998); *Arqueología de Buenos Aires* (1999)*; Historia del Comer y del Beber en Buenos Aires* (2000); *The Historical Archaeology of Buenos Aires* (2000)*; Buenos Aires Negra*

(2003); *El mural de Siqueiros en la Argentina* (2003); *Treinta siglos de imágenes* (2004); *Los conventillos de Buenos Aires: la Casa Mínima, un estudio arqueológico* (2005)*; La imagen de América* (2005)*; Túneles de Buenos Aires* (2005).

His publications include 250 papers in scientific and dissemination magazines worldwide. Since 1984 he has a tenure at the School of Architecture, Design and Urban Planning, University of Buenos Aires, and has been a professor in different universities across the Americas, particularly in México; he has also taught courses in Latin America, to Master and Ph.D. candidates. He has lectured and delivered papers at professional meetings. He is a member of several post-graduate academic committees.

He has been awarded prizes and fellowships from the Guggenheim Foundation (1994), the National Gallery of Art-CASVA (1995), the Graham Foundation for the Arts (Chicago, 1984), the Getty Grant Program (1991), Dumbarton Oaks (1996), the DAAD Berlin (1988), the Center for Latin-American Studies, University of Pittsburgh (2002), FAMSI (1995 and 2003), the Center for Compared Anthropology, University of Bonn (1998) and others. He was granted several national awards for his scientific achievements and his works concerning national heritage. He is Emeritus Advisor to the National Commission of Museums and Historic Monuments, a Member of the Academy of History, Buenos Aires, and its Secretary since 2005. He travels extensively throughout Latin America and the United States, and has resided in México for nine years.

Index

Abingdon Park (NYC), 92
Abingdon Square, 90
Acamapichtli (king), 14
Acosta, José, 14
Africa and Africans in the Making of the Atlantic World (Thornton), 34
African diaspora gardens, 29–40
    aesthetic, medicinal, and food purposes, 37
    Amerindian influences, 32
    dooryard gardens, 31, 34, 36, 39
    erosion control strategies, 38
    folklore and, 39
    foreign plant sources, 36
    horticultural innovations, 31
    knowledge and naming, 35–37
    multi-story cropping, *36,* 37–38
    origins and development of, 31–34
    political events and, 34
    provision grounds, 31–35, 38
    rituals and supernatural practices, 38–39
    spatial order and social control, 34–35
    subjectivity definition, 38–40
    techniques, 37–40
Alameda (poplar grove), 50, *50*
Alcántara Onofre, Saúl, 5, 7
Almácigos, 9, *21,* 21–22, *24, 26*
Alphand, Adolphe, 51, 90
American Southern Cone, 48
American War of Independence, 34
André, Edouard, 53, 54
Anonymous Conqueror, 13
Armstrong, Douglas, 39
Arnold, Samuel G., 68
Aztecs
    and *Chinampas,* 10
    in Iztacalco, 11
    settlements and mythical narratives, 4
    Tenochititlan, 11–17

Bachelard, Gaston, 4, 38
Baldi, Renzo, 66
Barbados, 35
Barillet-Deschamps, Jean-Pierre, 90
Bayles, J.C., 89
Benoît, Catherine, 5, 7
Berjman, Sonia, 5–6
Bernal-Garcia, Maria Elena, 4
Boermel, Carlos, 76
Bouvard, Joseph, 55–56
Buchanan, W.J., 79–80
Buenos Aires, Argentina. *See also* Buenos Aires (city) public parks and plazas
    as capital city, 53–57
    fragmentation and postmodernism, 58–60
    Haussmann-like plan for, 54
    immigration, 66
    modernity quest, 6, 58
    Parisian influence, 51–52
    population growth, 53, 58
Buenos Aires (city) public parks and plazas, 47–61. *See also* Palermo Park
    amusement architecture, 50
    Bouvard park plan, 55–56
    bullrings, 50
    "cement squares" *(plaza secas), 58,* 58–59
    democracy after 1983, 60
    democratization of public space, 56
    founding of city, 48
    France Square *(Plaza Francia),* 55
    French formal influence, 54–55, 56, 57, 60, 61
    homeless people and, 60, *60*
    Lezama Park, 55
    modernity quest, 6
    neo-Spanish revival, 57
    nova urbe concept, 48–49
    Plaza Mayor *(Plaza de Mayo), 49,* 49–50, *50, 52,* 55, 59–60
    plaza origin, 48
    Plaza Perú, *58*
    plazuelas (little plazas), 50
    social point of view, 56
    societal changes of 20th century and, 58
    U.S. influence, 57
Burial practices, of slaves, 39–40
Burnhap, George, 93

Cabrera, Miguel, 69, 74
Camaña, Juan, 69
Canal de la Viga, 10, *10,* 21
Canal Street Park (NYC), 90, *90,* 92
Canopy stratification, 37, 38
Careri, Gemelli, 16
Caribbean landscape, 29, 34. *See also* African diaspora gardens
Carrasco, Benito, 56
Central Park (NYC), 88, 94, 97
Chalco, Lake, 13, 18, 20, 21, 26, 27
Chapultepec, 13
Chinampas, 3, 9–27, *16, 19, 24*
    almácigos (earth/seed beds), 9, *21,* 21–22, *24, 26*
    basic characteristic of, 9
    chapines (plant cubes), *22*
    construction process, 17, 18–20
    contemporary situation, 17–18
    cultivation, 19–24
    dimensions, 19
    existing, *11,* 20–21
    flowers and, 24–25
    foundation of, 18–19
    historical survey, 11–17
    irrigation systems, 15, 23–24
    lessening of areas in Mexico City, 20–21
    map representations of, 25
    production, 10, 24–25
    protected management of, 11
    restored, *20*
    soil recycling, 23
    vegetables and, 25
    weather precautions, 22–23, *23*
    willow trees *Salix bonplandiana, 13,* 20, *20*
    word origin, 9
    with xacalli (house), *17*
    Xochimilco landscape origins, 25–27
Ciénega Grande, *15*
City model (modernization), 51–52

Civilization and Barbarism (Faustino Sarmiento), 52
Clavijero, Francisco Javier, 13, 16–17
Cominges, Juan de, 78
Commission to Select and Locate Lands for Public Parks, 88
Corlears Hook Park, 89, 90, *92,* 92–93, *93,* 94
Cortez, Hernán, 12–13, 16, 26
Courtois, Eugène, 54
Creole culture. *See also* African diaspora gardens
    cuisine, 37
    gardens and emergence of, 40

Dama Lasta, Ricardo, 66
Delle, James, 34
Descalzi, Nicolás, 69
Díaz, Porfirio, 21, 27
Díaz del Castillo, Bernal, 13
Disease, and congested urban areas, 89
Dooryard gardens, 31, 34, 36, 38
    phenomenology of, 39
Downing, Andrew Jackson, 98
Durá, Diego, 14, 16

East River Park, 89

Farm School Program, 97–99, *98*
    model homes and, 98
    and perception of public space and landscape architecture, 99
Faustino Sarmiento, Domingo, 52–53
Floating gardens. *See Chinampas*
Folklore, 39
Forestier, Jean Claude Nicolas, 57, 59
France Square *(Plaza Francia),* 55
French Encyclopedia Movement, 52

García Granados, Rafael, 16
García-Zambrano, Angel Julían, 4
Garden and Forest, 91
Gardens
    in development of identities/cultural forms, 40
    as a Fine Art, 4
    history and, 4
    identities in African diaspora, 31
    personality and, 6
    political circumstances in creation of, 5
    as representation of slavery, 40
    social or cultural functions of, 4
    symbolic of heritage politics, 40
Gilroy, Thomas, 90
Grand Tenochtitlan, Lake, 10
Grant, Hugh, 90
Guadeloupean gardens, 38, 40. *See also* African diaspora gardens
Gulick, Luther Halsey, 95, 97
Gutiérrez, Ramón, 73

Haciendas, 26
Haiti, 38, 40
Haussmann, Baron de, 51
Hernando de Ojeca, Fray, 14–15
Hewitt, Abram S., 89–90, 90, 100
Higman, Barry, 35
Hobsbawn, Eric, 57

Hodgepodges *(salmigondis),* 36
Humboldt, Alejandro de, 13

Iannaconne, Rachel, 6, 7
Immigrants, and public space, 87
Independence Centennial (Buenos Aires), 55
Independence Pyramid, 51–52
Iztapalapa, 16

Jamaica. *See also* African diaspora gardens
    burials of enslaved Africans, 39
    gardens, 38
Jeannette Park (NYC), 90, 92
Jefferson Park (NYC), 89
Jose de Urquiza, Justo, 66

Koch, Robert, 89

Landscape and myth, 4
Landscape architects, and public space, 87–88
Lee, Joseph, 95
Lezama Park, 55
Lower East Side Recreation Society, 99

MacCann, William, 67, 70
Makena, Vicuña, 71
Mar del Plata, Argentina, 55
Mauduit, Fernand, 77
McKee, Larry, 35
Medicinal plants, 37, 40
Methfessel, Adolf, 76
Mexico City
    Chinampas as source of vegetables and flowers in, 18
    early descriptions of *chinampas,* 16
    loss of *chinampas* areas in, 10, 20–21
    urban sprawl of, 18
Milpas. *See Chinampas*
Moles, Abraham A., 38
Montezuma, 13
Montpelier plantation, 35
Monument to Independence (Palermo), 66
Mulberry Bend Park (NYC), 89, 90, *90,* 93, 94, *94,* 95
Multi-story cropping, *36,* 37–38
Myth, and landscape, 4

Napoleon III, 51
National Recreation Movement, 95
Native American gardening techniques, 32
Newell, Timothy, 88
New York City small parks, 87–101
    Abingdon Square, 90
    Canal Street Park, 90, *90*
    Corlears Hook Park, 89, 90, *92,* 92–93, *93*
    East River Park, 89
    educational programs, 95
    Farm School Program, 97–99
    female educators' roles in, 98
    French influences on, 90–91
    Jeannette Park, 90
    Jefferson Park, 89
    Manhattan districts, 89

Mulberry Bend Park, 89, 90, *90,* 93, 94, *94,* 95
  music programs, 95–96, *96*
  need for "breathing spaces," 88
  playgrounds, 95, 99, 101
  as property and responsibility of users, 98
  public use debate, 88
  recreational programs and team sports, 95
  Seward Park, *100,* 100–101, *101*
  Small Parks Act, 89
  social control and "civilizing" of immigrants, 93–94
  St. Gabriel's Park, 101
  Tompkins Square Park, 96–97
  Van Cortlandt Park, 88–89
Noel, Carlos, 57

Oldendorff, Ernst, 77
Olmsted, Frederick Law, 91, 98
Outdoor Recreation League, 99, 100

Palermo Park, *53,* 53–53, *55, 57,* 65–83, *68, 69, 80, 81*
  antibarbarism symbol, 77
  Avenida del Libertador, 77
  Botanical Garden, 77
  Caserón, 68, 71–73, 75–76, 78–80
  creation of new park, 76–78
  documentary archive, 83
  early buildings, 70–71
  as expression of independence, 67–68
  factors in location choice, 67
  landscape changes, 77
  landscape design, 69–70
  main gates, *78*
  materialization of social success, 66
  national architecture and, 72–73
  orthogonal scheme, 70
  parks in poorer sections of Palermo, 81
  park use restrictions, 80–82
  post-Rosa design, 74–76
  private ownership of park lands, 82–83
  promenades, *81,* 82
  recuperation of floodable lands, 70
  Rosas political project, 66–74
  Sarmiento and, 76, 80–81
  sculptures and monuments, 65, 66
  societal changes and, 77
  Sordeaux plan, *73*
  use of, during Rosa regime, 74
  water systems, 71
Paris, France, 51–52
Parks, Promenades and Gardens of Paris, 91
Parque 3 de Febrero. See Palermo Park
Parson, Fannie Griscom, 97–99
Parsons, Samuel Jr., 90, 92, 99–101
Pasteur, Louis, 89
Peasant breach, 32
Plantations
  Brazilian, 34
  coffee, 34
  diversity of gardens and fields in, 31–32
  garden role in economics of, 30
  Great House gardens, 31
  Jamaican, 35
  land tenure, 34–35
  layout, 35
  Louisiana Evergreen plantations, 35
  provision grounds, 32–35
  sugarcane cultivation, 32–33
  types of fields in, 31
  Virginia, 35
Playgrounds (NYC), 95, 99, 101
Plaza Mayor *(Plaza de Mayo), 49,* 49–50, *50*
  Alameda (poplar grove), 50, *50*
  modernization of, 55
  protests by *Madres de Plaza de Mayo, 59,* 59–60
Poetics of Space (Bachelard), 38
Ponce, Fray Alonso, 15
Poplar Forest, VA, 37
Practice of Everyday Life (Certeau), 34
Price, Richard, 39
Promenades de Paris, Les, 91
Proto-peasantry, 32
Psychologie de l'espace (Moles and Rohmer), 38
Public space, and social change, 87–88
Pueyrredon, Prilidiano, 51–52

Querol, Agustín, 66

Ramirez codex, 14
Reformers, and public space, 87–88
Riis, Jacob, 90
Robinson, William, 91
Rocha, Héctor, 66
Rodin, Auguste, 66
Rohmer, Élisabeth, 38
Rosas, Juan Manuel de, 6
  destruction of home of, 78–80
  home built by, 66–67
  military defeat of, 75
  statue of, 66
Rosas, Manuelita, 71, *72*

St. Gabriel's Park (NYC), 101
Santos-Granero, Fernando, 4
Sarmiento, Domingo F., 6, 66, 69, 74, 80–82
Sartorio, José Santos, 73–74
Schavelzon, Daniel, 5–6, 7
Schiaffino, Eduardo, 71
Schilling, Elizabeth, 27
Self-identity, 4
Senillosa, Felipe, 73
Seward Park (NYC), *100,* 100–101
Slash-and-burn agriculture, 38
Slave economy, 32. *See also* African diaspora gardens
Slave gardens, 29–30. *See also* African diaspora gardens
  dooryard gardens, 31
  provision ground, 31–35
Small Park Advisory Committee, 90, 100
Small Parks Act, 89
Social change, and public space, 87–88
Social hygiene, 82
Soja, Edward, 34
Southern Arawaks, 4

Space
    cultural use of, 4–5
    garden space and formation of personality, 6
    spatial order and social control, 34–35
    symbolic value of, 3, 4, 6
    verticality of, 4
Stover, Charles, 99–101
Strong, William, 90
Symbolism, of space, 3, 4

Technical thinking, 3
Tenement House Reform, 88
Tenochititlan, 11–17
    landscape during conquest of, 12–17
    Montezuma, 13
Texcoco, Lake, 3, 5, 10
Thays, Carlos León (son), 56
Thays, Charles (Carlos) (father), 54–55
Thornton, John, 34
Tompkins Square Park (NYC), *96*
Torcuato de Alvear, 54
Toribio de Benavente, Fray, 16
Torquemada, 15
Trollope, Anthony, 29

UNESCO World Heritage Site, 11
Urban "hygiene," 52
Urbanism science, 56
Urquiza, Justo J. de, 74–75

Valley of Mexico. *See also* Aztecs; *Chinampas;* Xochimilco (city)
    beauty of landscape, 26
    Lakes Xochimilco and Chalco, 10, 13, 18, 20, 21, 26, 27
    water levels, 27
Van Cortlandt Park (NYC), 88–89
Van Rensselaer, Mariana, 91
VanWyck, Robert, 101
Vaux, Calvert
    design goals, 91–92, 93
    influences, 90–91
    philosophy, 91
Vetancurt (Franciscan Father), 16
"View in Old North Sound, Antigua" (Johnson), 30, *30*
Villas and Cottages (Vaux), 91

Waisman, Marina, 59
Western culture, and symbolism of space, 3, 4
World Heritage At-Risk List, 11
Wysoscki, Jordan Czeslaw, 76–77

Xochimilco, Lake, 10, 18, 20, 21, 26, 27
Xochimilco (city), 11, *11, 12,* 17
    declared World Heritage Site, 11
    hydrographic situation of, *18*
    landscape origins, 25–27
    urban layout of, 26
    viceroyal houses, 26–27